MW01173316

The Deliverance Project

A Seven Step Journey Toward True Freedom

J. Carroll-Flowers

ISBN-13: 978-1-881223-80-1

Printed in the U.S.A.

Contents

Expressing Gratitude

To my husband, Arvie, who through the years has been my best friend, my shoulder to lean on, my biggest fan, my spiritual coach, and whose love has meant everything to me. I love you!

To my daughters, Char and Joi, who continually inspire and motivate me to change the world.

To RJ, my grandson who continues to grow in the fruit of the Spirit; never let anyone or anything turn you around. You are truly an anointed messenger.

To my grandchildren, Frank, Kayla, Jeremiah, Elijah, Jayla, Briele, Darius, Dexter, Micah, Niarah, and Rheighn.

To Dom and Pam, Barbara and Reaves, Carolyn and Charles, Cheryl and Reggie, Yvonne and James, and Carole G. – the best friends anyone could ever have.

To my BFF Felicia, for her support and encouragement during my life-long journey to discover "self."

To Bishop Henry Fernandez, Senior Pastor at The Faith Center in Sunrise, who has shown me that "ordinary people CAN do extraordinary things by maximizing their potential." Thank you for being real!

And finally, to my spiritual family: Abba, my Father who is the source of my strength; Jesus Christ, my Lord and Savior; and the Holy Spirit, my personal advisor who gives me peace in times of so many storms. Thank you for the awakening.

Note From The Author

I hope you have chosen to do this study because you are seriously interested in experiencing a transformational change. Or perhaps you simply want to reinforce the change that has already taken place in your life. Whatever the reason, I'm glad you are joining me on this exciting journey.

My assumption is that you have already read *The People Zoo – A Guide To Know Who You're Talking To*. I believe you will gain more insight from Lemuel's fifty-year journey in and out of jails and prison. His story gives us a humorous, yet realistic account of what mass incarceration does to the human spirit. We can learn a lot from other people's experiences, as well as our own thoughts and actions.

The Deliverance Project is my follow up to *The People Zoo*. This seven-step journey takes a deep dive into our human existence as a spiritual being. From my experience, most churches don't do that. They recruit you, baptize you, and then leave you to your own understanding. Think about it. Believers go from church to church leaning on their emotions, rather than learning about their humanity. I'm glad I finally found a church that doesn't do that; a church that challenges me to live intentionally on a level beyond the physical world. It helps me to be faith centered.

I have learned that faith is all about trust. Without faith it's impossible to create a bond between the seen and the unseen, between the known and the unknown.

The truth is that we are more than what we visualize and believe to be real about ourselves as human beings. Yes, there is an outer body that we can see and touch, but there's also an inner being that is ruled by a supernatural force. Hopefully, this book will help you grasp a broader understanding of the fundamental principles of the creation of mankind and why we exist in this crazy mixed-up world.

My goal in writing this book is to help you have a different perspective of what you have always thought to be reality. Just because certain things are accepted without any question or doubt doesn't mean they are true.

A classic example is the man I wrote about in my book *The People Zoo – A Guide To Know Who You're Talking To*. Lemuel is an ex-offender who says, "A human being is not born just to eat, sleep, work, and play. This is the life of an animal." If a person sees himself as a victim of society, this view will shape the way he feels, thinks, talks, and acts within society. People become comfortable believing they are victims of situations and circumstances. Yet, our behavior is a function of our decisions, not our circumstances. This kind of thought pattern can only lead an individual down a path to failure in this journey called life. On the other hand, knowing the truth and accepting reality are two different paradigms. It's a process that must happen at a higher level of thinking. A level that relies on faith.

Everyone held in captivity wants to be free. But not every captive has the same view of what freedom means. Most people will say it's having the independence to do what you want without being restricted. This narrow view does not mean someone has the right to violate another person's rights. There are laws that prevent this from happening and violators lose their own right to be free. If I'm the offender, then I can't be the victim. That's a reality.

The point is this: freedom does not change circumstances that landed a person in jail or prison in the first place. In fact, freedom is not something anyone can take away. Our greatest power is the freedom of choice.

As you walk through this journey and gain understanding, choose to apply to your life what you learn. The first step is an awareness of your unique nature as a spiritual being. If you are not a good reader, join a group with a Deliverance Peer Coach or find someone with a willing heart to be your mentor. Focus on the content with an open mind. You'll be amazed at what will happen.

Nature of Mankind

There are many different views of how and when human beings were created. Scientific evidence shows our first ancestors appearing on earth between five and seven million years ago. Modern humans appeared in Africa within the past 200,000 years. What scientists can't agree on is when and how mankind transformed from ape-like creatures focused on survival and self-preservation into modern, creative human beings. The only evidence to support the historic theory of evolution comes from fossils, which are very sparse.

On the other hand, theologians don't believe mankind evolved from animals at all. The Biblical description of man's creation is a three-in-one being formed in the "image" and "likeness" of God. The Old Testament supports this view of the origin of man as a physical body with a living soul connected to a spiritual realm. In other words, human beings have 1) a physical body, 2) a soul that consists of the mind, emotions, and free will, and 3) a spirit that is eternally connected to a spiritual realm.

This book is not a study about religion. My book, *The People Zoo - A Guide to Know Who You're Talking To* was not written to start a debate about man's ancestry. The intent is to awaken the mind of my readers to the fact that we human beings are NOT descendants of animals. In *The Deliverance Project*, I present a distinct aspect of mankind as a three-in-one being. Adam and Eve were fully human, no matter how they were created. But they were also spirit before they became human bodies with a soul.

What's important is your understanding of natural laws that are part of an orderly universe. These laws exist outside of space and time, in the spiritual realm where unchanging principles are everlasting. Everything in creation has a preordained role related to its existence. The sun rises in the east and sets in the west. The moon has phases and lights up the night. Flowers bloom in spring and die in winter. It's the natural order of things.

So, it makes sense there are *true* principles that govern human development as well. Unlike anything else in creation, human beings have the free will to make their own life choices. But our decisions also have consequences which are beyond our control. Making the wrong choices is the essence of mental and spiritual growth. As humans we are supposed to learn from our mistakes.

In the context of natural law, human beings are created with a sense of "goodness" before we are born into the world. You probably don't understand this because right now you only see things from a worldly view. This is normal. But in Truth, we are spirit before we become a human body.

The seeds of compassion, empathy, and morality were placed in us before conception. Understanding and accepting the Truth about the nature of mankind will free you to practice a new way of thinking, which will result in a new way of living.

Scientists have found children know the difference between right and wrong before they reach the age of two. But to be *truly* good, a human being must be willing to sacrifice his or her own needs for the sake of others. That's a choice we make as individuals who adopt a pattern of life that is in perfect harmony with spiritual principles.

It's essential to recognize that we are all born with a human nature, just as we are all created with a moral conscience. As masters of our thoughts, we create our life situation in these thoughts. We become what we think.

The best way to understand the difference between our human nature and spiritual nature is to look at the lives of two different people. Imagine one mind that is dominated by thoughts of the flesh and the five senses, while the other mind is dominated by good thoughts and spiritual characteristics. You may already know two people like this who are opposites.

The person whose thought process is focused on "self" doesn't have the capacity to truly love others. Being *totally* human, this individual cannot *become* anything beyond his or her basic human nature of reacting with emotions. Everything is focused on "I" with conditions attached to every interaction with other people. In other words, this person's life is about **"What I want and need from YOU!"**

On the other hand, the person who lives from their *inner being* and is connected to the spiritual realm loves unconditionally. This person struggles to overcome their humanness and is constantly tempted by the ways of the flesh and the physical world. This person's life is focused on **"What do YOU want and need from Me?"**

On an even deeper level, the *inner being* of a good individual must continually be renewed on a daily basis. A person may go to church once a week to be revived, but that's hardly enough to overcome those old habits that can shift the mind to a false reality of survival. Bad things still happen to good people.

As I mentioned previously, the path ahead will take you into a new dimension of your being that will seem unfamiliar at first. It's the unseen that is difficult to accept. You will need a deeper level of trust as you face the unknown. Always remember that you are not alone.

With each step of this journey, you will be confronted with challenges that will grow you. Don't hesitate to decide what to do; which questions to answer; and what actions to take. Find your MY Space; rethink your habits and continue on your journey.

Quite often you will be tempted to stop. **DON'T!** Take a deep breath and relax. Tomorrow is another day.

Start Your Journey

This book is your guide through each of the seven steps on your journey to *Deliverance*. The background for this study is the laws of nature, which represent fundamental Truths. These natural laws or principles are self-evident in the environment and throughout the universe. We can argue about how natural principles are defined, especially when it comes to religion. But we can't deny that natural laws exist or change how these principles are governed. We can't block nature, and we can't stop nature. What we *can* do is take a deep dive to understand how the laws of nature impact human life, either positively or negatively.

There's a natural order of development for everything in creation. The acorn becomes an oak tree. The caterpillar becomes a butterfly. And the human infant grows into a child and then becomes an adult. Everything in creation has a purpose to move from one level to the next and is fully functional. Life is, by nature, a physical process obviously designed with supernatural genius.

What makes human beings different from other living creatures is the part of us that is not physical – the soul and the spirit. Although all three are connected, each element is distinctively different. Physical growth happens on the outside, while the soul and the spirit develop on the inside. One is an outward process while the other two are an inward process. This is true for every human being even if we aren't aware of it. The unknown is as real as the known.

Have you ever wondered why humans have a natural ability to read and write? Animals can't do that. Scientists have discovered that the brain of newborn babies is prewired to learn words later in life. Learning is a spiritual principle that links to the soul. What do I mean by that? Allow me to explain what is known.

Our soul can be defined as our consciousness: the aspects of life that combine the mind, free will, and emotions. Each of these components has its own purpose in the growth and development of our humanity. Let's look at the soul more closely.

Information, which comes from an outside source, is processed in the brain, where our feelings, emotions, and critical thinking take place. We can't see this process with the naked eye, but we know it exists. We except this as Truth because of scientific evidence.

Our body interacts and connects the brain with the physical world, which in turn influences how we think, feel, and react to different situations. The invisible soul is continuously developing with every experience, whether good or bad. It is the soul that reflects our individual personality.

Spirituality refers to knowing there is more to being human than reacting to our five senses of taste, sight, touch, hearing and seeing. That's the life of an animal. If all that we have is just a body, then mankind is no different than the rest of creation.

Our spirit center is the innermost, deepest part of our being that gives meaning and purpose for life. It connects us to a spiritual realm that is infinite, endless, and impossible for our human mind to measure or to imagine. Part of letting mankind know that a spiritual realm exists is our ability to explore its principles and to experience its supernatural power.

Maximizing our potential on earth comes from a spirit-centered dwelling place. I define spirituality as tapping into the deepest aspect of our humanness, which is unseen.

I believe the few weeks that you spend in this study will open your mind to a new way of thinking. Just remember there is no such thing as a quick fix to circumstances. Transformation is a fundamental change in your thoughts, which will affect your heart, and the way you approach life. You must be faith-centered in the unseen. Change can only come from your spirit center – working from the inside to respond to everything that happens to you on the outside.

In the end, your true self will come into *being* and you will see beyond your reflection in the mirror and what everyone else is looking at. Life will look less complex and make more sense if you read this book one step at a time.

Step One is an awakening that will take you back to the womb. Before you were born, you were a spirit and then you became human flesh. The intention in this step is to give you a balanced perception of your *true* self. There is a difference between your human nature and your spirit nature. Your *true* being was developed in the natural state of your creation.

Step Two closely examines relationships you have formed throughout your life. It is through the soul that people relate to each other. Every interaction with other human beings has either moved you forward or pushed you back. Once you understand how the human nature of relationships can build you up or put you down, you will make better choices in how you interact with others. The purpose of this step is to balance your perception of relationships, so you better understand the value of connections that come from the heart.

Step Three explores the workings of the soul – your thoughts, feelings, and freedom to choose. The purpose of this step is to help you recognize that your human experience is messed up. It's not a matter of bad habits, negative thoughts, and "happy pills." It's about your soul being out of alignment with your true self. For restoration to take place, the trash stored up in your soul needs to go.

Restoration is an inner process that requires trusting in the unknown and the unseen. Breaking habits is not an easy task. To become a "whole" person, you need to have unity with your body, mind, and spirit.

Step Four deals with conflict and feelings. In order to function successfully in today's world, it's necessary to have a deeper knowledge of how the mind, emotions, and free will work in response to difficult situations. How we think and feel determines how we react to situations. The hardest part is taking the time and energy to think things through. It's critical to understand that emotions can only affect you to the extent you react to situations.

We are all created in the thoughts that generate in our mind. In other words, our "being" becomes what we think. This is a natural principle of growth. Each individual must rely on *self* to build their own emotional intelligence.

Step Five looks at human life from a spiritual perspective, so you can see beyond human behavior and attitude. This step is important to perceive yourself as having value and self-worth. It means deep thinking about the way you do things. If you don't respect yourself, then you can't expect other people to give you respect.

It's not what you do that makes you who you are, but who you are that makes you do what you do.

As you read through this step you will be reminded to check your behavior and attitude to see if they align with your *true* character. It's through your spirit connection that your soul guides you to become a better person, to have hope and to heal.

Step Six is a divine discovery of the talents and gifts that you were given during your natural creation, before your human birth. The key is to use these natural abilities to improve your life situation in the physical realm. Why is this important? Because without a life purpose you will continue to go around in circles, never making progress as time passes you by.

Research has found that people who lack a rich sense of purpose have significantly worse mental and physical health. This step doesn't offer a science-based strategy to answer the question of why you were born. But it will help you discover an in-dwelling source of power to take you to a much higher level of thinking, so you can experience life on a new level of awareness. The seed is already planted in every human being to live a purposeful life. Who you are is why you exist. By gaining a greater self-awareness you will find purpose for your physical life.

Knowing how to improve your earthly situation is called wisdom and it comes from the spiritual realm, which is in you and always with you. Becoming aware of this higher power and using it to change your life for the better is what fulfilling your purpose means. Doing this is not as difficult as you may think.

Step Seven is your guide to a lasting breakthrough if you really desire to be a more effective person. It's a choice.

A very important element of your soul is free will, as far as our conscious mind is concerned. Dealing with life in the physical realm affects how we think, feel and act. Most people are trapped in the belief they can't control their own lives. What we can't control is the consequences of our decisions. Making the right choices usually results in the right actions.

Although we are humans, we were created in the spirit before we were created as physical beings. Only with acceptance of this Truth can you begin to experience the existence of a spiritual realm. There are important elements to lasting peace that can only come from the inside to be lived on the outside. This final step is actually a new beginning. It will help you to see yourself in a new light and motivate your spirit to action.

That's the difference *real* knowledge and understanding can make. Unfortunately, our Western culture places far too much emphasis on developing the outer person and not enough on growing the inner being.

You can't expect to reap positive results in life from negative thoughts. The natural laws of the spiritual realm simply don't work that way. Oneness can only occur when the mind, body and spirit exist in perfect harmony. The mind only knows what it understands. When we find it within ourselves to seek Truth, an invitation comes from the spiritual realm. What happens next?

There is a pull on every heart that we are unable to deny. Some people ignore it, while others answer the call and follow their heart.

A structured plan can help to keep your mind focused on learning. You will also need a quiet place to study. What I mean by "study" is taking the time to learn something by reading and focusing on the meaning of what you read. The challenge is to read one step a week and complete the activities. Again, if you are not a good reader get someone to read with you or start a "Deliverance Project" group with people who have the same common goal. This will keep you from feeling overwhelmed while being motivated by others to learn.

If you need more time to complete a step, take it. Reading this book is not about joining a marathon race. One step a week is only a suggestion, it's not a rule. Just remember to replace negative thoughts with positive ones. If you hear yourself thinking "I can't do this," stop and change that thought to "I CAN do this!" Don't allow yourself to make excuses.

The Seven Steps in this book worked for me. I believe they will help to set the stage for a balance of your mind, body, and spirit to occur. So, don't let *The Deliverance Project* sit on a shelf to collect dust. Take the first step and stay the course. Refer back to the activities often to monitor your progress. Believe in yourself and trust the journey. Lasting change can only happen if you are motivated and determined to make it happen.

Step One - Awareness
The Substance of Your Being

Before starting this step, find a quiet "My Space" to read. If there are two or more people in the study, create a "We" space.

Take at least 10 minutes to meditate and relax. Slowly breathe in, hold your breath for three seconds, and breathe out. Breathe in, hold for three seconds, and breathe out. Breathe in, hold for three seconds, breathe out. This will help to increase your concentration.

Now, close your eyes and imagine the peace and serenity you experienced while you were in the womb, being provided for and protected in a spiritual reality. This is your first awareness of yourself as a living spirit in a physical world.

Once you are relaxed and ready to focus, spend the next 60 minutes reading, writing, and thinking. All you need is 60 minutes a day, five days a week to learn something new. When you finish this step, read it again. According to science, our brain recalls in three stages. So, it's okay to take longer than a week for each step.

The purpose of this first step is to take you beyond the physical concept of life; beyond gratification of your five senses. This step will give you a balanced perception of your *true* self as spirit in a human body. What you learn needs to stay with you. The idea is to understand more about *self* and to retain what you read.

A catholic priest and philosopher, Pierre Teilhard de Chardin said, "We are not human beings having a spiritual experience. We are spirit beings having a human experience." [1] Consciousness is merely awareness of our internal and external existence.

We all know there is "something' supernatural at work in the universe, but we don't know what that "something" is. In trying to make sense of creation, we tend to view everything in human terms. It's hard to explain what we can't see or hear or touch.

Science has discovered there are two very important aspects of our human existence: **matter** and **substance**. Everything is made of matter, even humans. Rather than us disagreeing on semantics, let's be clear how this book defines matter and **substance**.

Everything that exists in the physical world is composed of tiny particles that occupy physical space. If it has mass and takes up space, then the substance is a form of matter. This is known science. Examples of different kinds of matter are a cell phone, a banana, a car, and a human being. It all depends on the way the tiny particles come together. Scientists break matter down into three different categories of substance: solids, liquids, and gases. Matter is the substance of what things are made of, even when matter changes into different forms. For example, if you boil water it turns into gas. Look at matter this way: things don't **consist of matter**; they **exist in matter**. When water boils, it doesn't vanish. It simply changes from one form to another.

Name six examples of matter that is either solid, liquid, or gas. For example, oxygen is a gas.

1. Gas: _____

2. Solid:_____

3. Liquid: _____

4. Gas: _____

5. Liquid: _____

6. Solid: _____

The scientist, Albert Einstein said: *"Energy cannot be created or destroyed; it can only be changed from one form to another."* [2]

What this means is a supernatural, omnipotent, omnipresent Spirit exists in matter, and it can never die. This Spirit simply changes matter into a different form within its own existence. This supernatural presence exists everywhere and is in everything and is stronger than what we know as death.

Substance is matter which becomes tangible and has a material presence. Human beings have physical bodies that were formed in matter. The primary substance of the human body is protein, which is the main component of our muscles, bones, organs, skin, and nails. As human beings, we have a tangible, solid presence in the physical world that was created in highly organized matter.

In the Bible, David proclaims in Psalms 139:14, *"I praise you, for I am fearfully and wonderfully made."*

David is a fascinating character in Scripture who recognized a supreme being who created the uniqueness and complexity of his human body and everything else in the universe. He was the author of many of the Psalms in the Old Testament. Now, all of this may seem a bit philosophical, but it's *Truth*.

Science uses observation to explain and justify any natural phenomena. However, scientists can't observe the supernatural and therefore have difficulty proving it. There's no scientific way to gather evidence about the laws of nature that are outside and beyond the realm of science. Humans don't have the capacity to explain the force that holds the universe together, although we try. The knowledge of scientists is confined to explaining the existence of matter; but only to the limit of what it does, not where it comes from or the powerful spirit within it.

Scientists have ideas about how the universe began. You've probably heard of the "Big Bang" theory. But there is always the question of *what happened before that?* Keep in mind, scientists are human beings who make assumptions based on their limited knowledge. They collect evidence and call their findings fact. They also describe supernatural powers as part of the laws of nature. The fact these laws or principles have authority over all matter and substance in the universe…and beyond…is evidence that there is something greater than science.

The reason I believe in a "Godhead," is because science can't prove that it's NOT true.

As a child I accept the fact that I have a Spirit Father who is perfect in power, wisdom and goodness. A deity who created the universe and loves everything in it – including me.

Many people, myself included, are deceived by our eyes and act on assumptions rather than facts. Then, we delve deeper and discover there's more to the situation than meets the eye. It's human nature to only believe what we can see. Especially if we are more closely connected to a worldly system than we are to the spirit realm. We all believe what we see and strive to understand what we don't see. Anyone can have doubts, but that does not mean there's no such thing as a "Supreme Being." Choice is a human initiative as well as an act of our spirit nature.

Anyone looking for a deeper understanding of spiritual reality can look at life from a scientific perspective. As humans, we consist of substance and our matter is not limited by a physical body. Emotions we feel are real. We can't see the air we breathe, yet it is necessary for life. We can't see ideas and thoughts, but we *can* see the results of actions that are generated by them. There is *real* evidence of the existence of a higher order that is connected to the things that we see, hear, feel, taste, and touch. Spirit is in matter.

Your life didn't start with a thrust from the womb into an uncertain world. You had a conscious spiritual identity before you were placed in the womb. You existed as an *idea* in spirit matter before you existed in the natural realm. You existed as a *spirit being* prior to conception; before you became a *biological being*.

No human is self-created. We don't form ourselves in the womb. We exist as energy in the spirit realm to be transformed into substance that eventually comes into *being* in the natural world. Before you were planted into a womb to become flesh you were spirit. Think about creation this way. Just as the acorn was spirit before it transitioned into substance, it had the capacity to become an oak tree. The idea already existed. What do you think happens to the embryo in the womb? Spirit matter in its purest form is destined to transition into a *human being with a living soul.*

I am fully convinced that human life begins in the spirit realm as a spirit that is without form. I know this may sound strange, but humans are a spirit that exists in substance. And when we are born into the world, we still exist in a spiritual form that was transitioned into a body of bones, flesh, and organs. The soul (emotions, mind, and free will) existed in a higher dimension before being placed in the human embryo to develop and grow from childhood to adulthood in human form.

To better understand this concept, let's start with the basics. Everything in the universe is matter, that much is known to be Truth. There's a place called the spirit realm where everything natural is first created as an *idea*. From this "center," everything is continuously being created to grow into the fullest of its being.

Because we know so little about the spirit realm, let's define it as supernatural intelligence. If you are religious, then you know this supernatural being as a deity and there is only one supernatural being that exists in all matter and substance. Without this "Godhead" there would be no matter or substance.

The essence of Spirit matter is divine love, which means to be deeply connected and committed to something unseen. Divine love precedes the existence of substance and therefore, divine love precedes our human existence. That leaves the question of where did we all come from before our conception?

Scientifically, your physical body began with the union of the sex cells from a human mother and a human father. You were *in* the world living in a womb, but you were not yet consciously *of* the world. It's very important to understand and believe this concept of human reality to discover your **true** self.

Once fertilization happens, growth and development of all life is totally dependent on the laws of nature and a Spirit Father.

There are a variety of scientific and religious opinions about when life begins. The question always comes up: *At what point does the spirit being become a human being?*

I personally believe it's at the point of conception, but there are other opinions that I also respect. I don't want to get into the "pro-life" verses "women's rights" debate, so let's not go there. That's not what *The Deliverance Project* is about. I simply want to make a point that every individual pops into existence in matter before we become substance in the womb.

We are an invisible spirit that becomes a human cell during conception. In bringing my mind to an awareness of this phenomenon, the starting point for me was a revelation within my conscious mind. Something supernatural happened in the spirit realm that connected with me in the physical world.

Now, let's return for a moment to the image of you in your first home – your mother's womb. There you are, unborn, with a spirit-based agenda you cannot control. Did you know that everything you will become in the physical world starts in the spirit realm? You first existed as spirit in matter and then your substance was formed as an idea. In other words, before you grew up in your mother's womb you already existed as the person you are now, including the color of your skin, the texture of your hair, your height at maturity, the color of your eyes, the shape of your face, and so forth. But you were destined to become more through life experiences in a physical world.

There's a DNA blueprint that followed a natural principle during your creation. I hope you can grasp this Truth about your true identity as a spiritual being implanted into a woman's womb with a soul to develop and grow. My personal theory is that matter and supernatural love are linked to the spirit realm.

Look at life this way. The Spirit matter, which is pure and without blemish, needs a home. Although the soul and spirit are independent, both also needs a home. Both dwell and interact within the human body. This is your reality in its simplest form.

Before we move on, let's see what you've learned so far. Circle True or False to the five questions on the next page.

1. Our true self-image is mind, body, and spirit.   True   False

2. Animals can change their nature.   True   False

3. Nothing is above the authority of the spirit realm.   True   False

4. Love means to be deeply connected to something.   True   False

5. Before you became human you were spirit first.   True   False

Perhaps the most important learning from this step is that your transformation was a natural occurrence where matter turned into physical substance in the comfort of your mother's womb. You still existed before conception, only in a different form.

It's virtually impossible for a human being to break the laws of nature. Mankind has a natural relationship to these principles, meaning our nature is to be obedient to the authority of the spirit realm. You can't recall the experience of a single cell replicating into billions of cells to create your human body. But the mere fact that you are alive is evidence of a supernatural process that finds pleasure in transforming itself into things that are wonderfully made. That is the essence of love you experienced in your mother's womb, through a connection with your Spirit Father. Your mind can't recall it because the experience was your soul and spirit being "fearfully and wonderfully made" within a human body.

What if you could describe the love of your first experience with the supernatural? Research has discovered that a fetus can express itself while going through the process of *becoming*. A machine called an ultrasound allows doctors to see babies in their natural state – crying, laughing, smiling, frowning, and even sucking their thumb. Not only does the fetus float, it responds to light and sound, moves about, eats, sleeps, and opens and shuts its eyes. The unknown is captured in pictures.

What we see happening on an ultrasound becomes *Truth*. So, before you can understand your *true* self, you must understand where you came from. During your time in the womb, you developed a unique parental relationship with your Spirit Father. This is true of everything in the earth that has life. The difference in the life of mankind is the ability to create, to communicate, to have awareness of a spirit relationship and be empowered by it.

Close your eyes and imagine what it must have been like in a space of divine love where you were not in control. Like the lilies growing in the field, you were in harmony with the laws of nature, experiencing the joy of becoming you. In this peaceful state of transcendence, you were *in* the world, but you are not *of* the world. It was a wonderful place that you never wanted to leave, because in the spirit realm you were connected to the very source of all life, joy, happiness, and divine love.

Now, imagine being thrust into a cold world where you must make smart choices to survive. Your birth date was a complex experience, both traumatic and frightening. It was a moment in your life when you suddenly became aware that everything around you had changed. You were separated from the womb.

At birth, a t different awareness takes place for every human. Life in the womb is total surrender to a supernatural authority. Love is the essence of our being because we don't know anything else. A human being has value by the simple fact that each of us is created in the image and likeness of our supernatural Father. The ultimate gift of this love is the ability to have inner freedom. Nothing else on earth has this gift. We are a unique creation.

A flower, for instance, not only has a natural beauty and a wonderful fragrance, but a supernatural energy that moves it from a seed to a bud to a blooming plant. Although unaware, the flower experiences the joy of *becoming*. The flower does not have the ability to change what it becomes. Now, imagine the joy when a human being becomes aware of this gift of a spirit nature and uses it for good in the world. At our very root we experience joy.

This is why history is full of ordinary people who have done extraordinary things. Scripture says mankind is created in the "image and likeness of God," which simply means we humans are formed in the essence of goodness and unconditional love.

Remember, the spirit is transformed into substance that takes on a human form. During the process of creation, the soul is designed with certain innate characteristics and qualities that are aligned with the spirit realm. In the womb, the soul exists in its purest form, free from negative thoughts, anxious feelings, and poor choices. Like a flower, our *true* self grows in its most wonderful and purest form. The reality, then, is that it is better for our true self to exist in the world. Our creation is, in turn, completed when our true self living in an earthly world can overcome evil thoughts and conquer temptations of the body through a spiritual connection.

Let me explain. For one thing, we come into the world already conscious of inner freedom. Our human *nature* allows us to make our own decisions. Remember, the body has a soul, which consists of a mind, emotions, and free will. I can't emphasize this point enough: what makes *human beings* different from everything else in creation is our ability to reason and an inner freedom to make choices. Think about this. You have control over your own destiny.

Can you see why there is conflict between body, soul, and spirit? Before we go any further, let's make certain you understand the difference between our human nature and our spirit nature. In the womb we trusted something supernatural that not only created us, but also grew us. Because we didn't know anything else, love in its purest form was given and received. We were *spirit beings* having our first experience as *human beings*.

A totally different awareness happened when we were born into the physical world. The soul is no longer suppressed. During the birthing process of the body, the spirit and soul were separated from the spirit realm. In this new awareness, coupled with our human nature, the body is perceived as a separate entity. There is also a disconnect of awareness of our true self as spirit.

With the awakening of the soul (the mind, emotions, and free will), the human becomes aware of an inner freedom to make choices, although without any knowledge and understanding of the consequences that come with free will. The power of the spirit realm is still available to any of us, but tapping into this link is a choice that requires learned knowledge and applied wisdom.

The spirit and soul are weakened with increased awareness of things of a worldly nature. Consequently, the subconscious mind tends to focus on self and material things. There's so much pressure to have a certain worldly image and to buy unnecessary things.

Of course, there's nothing wrong with wanting to have a nice car or a nice appearance. But as a society that values people by how much they earn or own, we tend to want more than we need. From a spiritual perspective, our desires, thoughts, emotions, and actions reflect what is going on in the soul. Some of us live life with the illusion that material things will make us happy. Believe me, I've been there. Our actions arise out of these thoughts, and we react without taking time for critical thinking. Without spiritual balance, the bad choices we make will always have negative consequences.

Think about your own life. What areas have kept you from the contentment you experienced before birth, in the spirit realm?

Acknowledging who you are is the first step to self-discovery. Habits are the actions we regularly perform every day. As we continue this journey, only *you* can decide whether to keep doing the same things that get you nowhere. Going down a different path is a matter of choice. Name five bad habits you would like to change.

1. _____

2. _____

3. _____

4. _____

5. _____

The most important question you will ever have to answer in life is who you are—not what others say about you, but what you believe about yourself. There's a vast difference between how most of us see ourselves and the underlying characteristics that make us who we really are as individuals. Think of all the baggage that is weighing down your soul, allowing confusion, misery, frustration, disillusion, and discouragement to reign. Is that the life you want?

The truth is negative habits have become so much a part of our culture that we simply don't know how to explore the inner life. We have lost touch with reality, believing every lie our ears hear; acting out every negative thought that comes to mind. Think about it. What are you doing for the people you say you love?

A critical moment in our human experience is when we come to realize our existence is simply a reduction of what our *real* life represents. There's a powerful force within us that keeps pulling us back to the spirit realm. If you look in a mirror, what do you see? At first glance you see yourself and your surroundings. But look deeper. Although everything appears to be the same, the images in the mirror are reflected backward. If you throw a ball at the mirror, you will actually see a reflection of it coming back toward you, retracing the path it travelled. If you want to see the image that you had in mind, that the ball is coming *from* you, then you have to do the opposite and throw the ball *to* yourself rather than *away* from yourself. The image in the mirror is not true.

Let's look at a different example. Take a moment to think about contemporary music. The words are usually focused on sex. The mind sees it, feels it, understands it, and draws actions from it. When this is done over and over again, habits are formed in the mind. Sex becomes something that is valued, and the mind seeks to live the experience that is imagined. It's no wonder the greatest conflict of our time is embodied in sexual immorality. Society has come up with so many excuses to accept ridiculous sexual behavior.

What should strike us at once is the fact that mankind is out of touch with the values, morals and convictions that build strong families and communities. Values are developed when we come into a deeper understanding of the goodness and power of a strong spirit. When we make a commitment to reconnect with the spirit realm, we become conscious of the correct and incorrect way to manage our existence in the physical world. Our soul (mind, emotions, and will) is then guided in the right direction for the body to enjoy the fruits of the Spirit. We'll talk about sowing and reaping in Step Two.

Right now, let's focus on how self-discovery is accomplished. There's only one path that lets you know who you really are. It's by removing human focus and centering your thoughts on spiritual principles. Do you know why everything that exists is constantly changing? It's because spiritual principles are rooted in reality. These basic Truths represent the way things are, always have been, and always will be. They are principles that run through the fabric of everything that exists. They have triumphed over millions of years. That's what makes the Bible so instructive. It's the "living word" that comes from the spirt realm.

There can be no wisdom, guidance, or personal power without understanding the underlying principles of spirit-centered living. The more you learn about these principles, the more clearly you will see the "fullness" of your creation. The image you see in the mirror is NOT your reality. Your *true* self-image can only be defined from the depths of your inner being, from your soul and your spirit; from the inside out.

Socrates was a Greek scholar, teacher, and philosopher who shaped the cultural and intellectual development of the world. One of his most famous quotes is: "To find yourself, think for yourself." Ironically, Socrates professed not to know anything important, but to seek answers through questions and dialogue. His method was to engage people in public conversations about man's human nature. Socrates motivated his audiences to think.

Socrates paved the way for other prominent ancient Greek thinkers like Aristotle and Plato. In fact, he was the first thinker in Western history to focus on self-discovery: who we are; what we are; who we should be; and what we become. He was an ordinary human being with extraordinary ideas. Where do you think his ideas, knowledge and inspiration originated from?

Socrates died in 399 BC (Before Christ) before any writings of books in the New Testament. Many of Socrates beliefs in human nature and his teachings were founded through observation and not scientific study. He taught that humans have an invisible soul that is eternal, and we are born with spiritual knowledge of what is true and moral. Socrates believed in a living soul that is eternal and never dies. His theory is that our souls and bodies are connected, but they are separate entities. Sound familiar?

If the soul determines what we feel and what we think, then why isn't the human body striving for perfection? The answer is simple. Once a human being is born into the physical world it's impossible for the human body to be perfect. Mankind's human nature is to gravitate toward the physical, toward things that are seen and heard. Our human nature wants things that can be enjoyed through the five senses, while our spirit nature influences us from the center of our being, which is on the inside.

Self-knowledge is all about getting to know yourself and loving who you are. You can't expect someone else to love you if you don't love yourself. Before you can set realistic goals, you must first know who you are.

What are your likes and dislikes? What are your values?

Everyone has a personality. It all boils down to which nature rules your life and mind – human nature or spirit nature. These two natures are opposites – one is carnal and the other is agape love, which is love in the highest form. Agape love seeks the well-being of others above love of self, no matter how others respond.

Understanding Yourself

Take a moment to think about who you really are as a person. Complete the activity below. In each Reality Check column put **ONE** check mark next to the Nature that best describes you or what people who know you best would say about you. Check either Human Nature or Spirit Nature ONLY, not both.

REALITY CHECK	HUMAN NATURE		SPIRIT NATURE	
Individual Responsibility	The only person I am responsible for is me.		I feel responsible to help people in need.	
Your Personality	I'd rather be alone than deal with diverse people.		I keep an open mind when meeting and working with diverse people.	
Your Relationships	I want benefits out of my relationships.		Love means no strings or conditions are attached.	
Your Motivation	I want to make a lot of money so I can make myself happy.		I want to fulfill my life's purpose so I can enjoy the fruit of the Spirit.	
Your Commitment	I keep a promise as long as I can benefit.		People trust me to do what I promise I will do.	
Your Habits	I hang on to bad habits to feel better.		I control bad habits so I can have a better quality of life.	
Your Attitude	I will get what I want in life by any means necessary.		I will survive in life without sacrificing my character or my spirituality.	
Your Abilities	I brag about my talents and skills.		I use my unique abilities to be of value to others.	
Your Values	I work hard and feel that I deserve all that I can get.		I find joy in putting the needs of others above my own needs.	
Your Behavior	When I'm offended, I don't get mad, I get even.		I forgive people who offend me and wish them well.	
Your Goals	I don't have any life goals; I just go with the flow.		I have short-term and long-term goals to accomplish during my life.	

What Would You Change?

The essential focus of the Reality Check is YOU. This exercise provides a mirror image of how you think and behave.

Now, focus on where you are in this season of your life. Whether young, old, or somewhere in between you have become what you think. Look at each Reality Check. Was it predominately your Human Nature or your Spirit Nature that got you where you are at this particular time in your life?

_____

If you could change something in the Human Nature column, what would it be and why?

_____

_____

_____

_____

Explain how change(s) you noted could affect the outcome of your current living situation and make a difference in your future.

_____

_____

_____

_____

_____

Step Two - Relationships
They Can Make or Break You

Before starting this step, find a quiet "My Space" that you can use while focusing on something that will calm your mind.

Take at least 10 minutes to relax. Close your eyes and slowly breathe in, hold your breath for three seconds, and breathe out. Breathe in, hold it for three seconds, and breathe out. Breathe in, hold it for three seconds, and breathe out. Think about how it truly feels to be loved unconditionally, without fear of being hurt.

You will get a lot more out of this journey if you take time to prepare your mind and body to unite with your spirit. Once you are completely relaxed, spend the next 30 minutes reading and writing. Remember, all you need is 30 minutes a day, five days a week to learn something new. When you finish, take time to read and review this step again. If it takes you longer than a week, no problem. You are learning something new and need to retain what you learn.

In the last step, you completed a "Reality Check" to get to know yourself better. Look back to see how often you checked the Human Nature column. It's okay if you put yourself first. You need to feel secure in knowing who you are now before visualizing yourself in a new way.

Self-awareness is all about understanding *self* – your behavior, responses, and choices, as well as the rewards and the consequences that come with the decisions you make.

Biologically speaking, a woman's womb is a wonderful place to live. You and everyone else had an amazing prenatal experience in an atmosphere of unconditional love. Even before conception, each of us had a close encounter within the spirit realm that was an incredibly loving and caring experience. Our very first relationship was an amazing spiritual love connection with our Creator.

In the womb, a love relationship flows from the mother to the fetus and from the fetus to the spirit realm. Our natural instinct is a sense of wanting to "belong." In cases where the mother is a drug user or an alcoholic, physical growth does not stop, even under stressful conditions. Love flows from the spirit realm to protect the fetus, even in difficult circumstances.

This love connection will be difficult to understand without accepting the fact that you are more than a body. I am going to say this repeatedly until you get it. Human beings are body, soul, and spirit. The body, which can be seen, is made of flesh and bones.

The soul is invisible and consists of emotions, which are your feelings, a mind that is housed in the brain and allows you to think, and a will that gives you freedom of choice to make decisions. Each of these elements is a separate entity but are connected through the flow of love from the spirit realm. A body, soul, and spirit is not what you have, but who you really are.

Evidence of the reality of a spirit realm is everywhere. It's the dominating authority over everything that is visible and invisible. It's an order of existence that can't be explained by science or the laws of nature. It's a love connection far beyond anything our human mind can understand, yet we must acknowledge our total dependence on it. Not understanding this connection between the body, soul, and spirit limits our ability to enjoy life in its fullness.

You may be thinking, "This sounds a lot like religion." No, this is Truth. Religion is an organization born out of Truth. Religion can teach you about the spirit realm, but it can't make that connection for you. A logical question that follows is: Where is this dominant power that has authority over everything in the universe? How can I find it?

If you don't know the answer, well then perhaps you didn't understand the message in Step One. Let me remind you that all things are created twice. There's the vision first and then comes the reality. First the spirit and then the physical.

Awareness that you were spirit first leads to knowledge that your body will die, but your spirit will still exist. It returns to its source.

Your transformation into a human was a natural process that turned matter into substance in the comfort and security of the womb. You existed before conception, but in a different form.

Nothing can ever separate you from the miraculous love connection you experienced before you were a human being. That's not to say that a love connection with your mother didn't begin almost immediately upon conception. Of course it did. You don't remember, but during your womb life you didn't take care of yourself. The human body is not self-created. There's an orderly process to human development that lasts about 40 weeks, whereby a physical mother and a Spirit Father work as a team.

You and your mother shared both a natural and a supernatural relationship. You ate what your mother ate; drank what she drank and reacted to her moods with a kick or two. And just as you depended on your mother for a healthy, full-term pregnancy, you also depended on your supernatural Father to prepare you for a worldly life. Let's look deeper into this love connection.

While your mother was making choices to ensure your fetal development, your Spirit Father was busy putting your structure in place; forming your brain, developing organs, bones, arms and legs, hands and feet, fingers, and toes and whatever else is physical.

Everything you are today was already created before you were born. Your life was preplanned so you could experience the world for yourself. Your ability to see, hear, smell, feel and taste are the same traits that animals possess. What makes humans different from everything else in the known universe is the ability to think and to reason. These traits, inherited from our Spirit Father are basic to all of mankind. We are prepared in the womb to live in a physical world through the power of a spiritual connection to our body, soul, and spirit. We are created with a soul (mind, emotions, and free will) to have authority over plants and animals.

Think of this gift as your inheritance. I will say it again: you were spirit before you became flesh. That means you had and still have a relationship with a Spirit Father that is a higher order of authority and consciousness than anything you can ever imagine. Through self-awareness that no human being is perfect, combined with a vision to be a better person, you can be empowered to make change happen.

Through imagination, you can grasp the important difference between the roles your "three" parents played in your creation. Your biological father provided the fertilization. Your biological mother carried you in her belly for nine months. But the stages of growth to prepare you for life in a physical world came from a more powerful, supernatural source.

Your growth from a single egg involved a much deeper, miraculous journey; something that is far beyond human control. You may or may not know your biological father, but your Spirit Father is an awesome, unconditional love connection rooted in *Truth*. A better, deeper understanding of the relationship with your Spirit Father will help you gain a greater knowledge of what path in life makes the most sense for you. Afterall, every parent wants what's best for their child.

I believe one of the most inspiring accounts of human life can be found in the Scriptures. The basic idea of a Spirit Father has been a topic of controversy for thousands and thousands of years. For our purpose of an awakening, I will use the Holy Bible as reference. Why? Because I believe this collection of books, some written over 3,500 years ago by ordinary people, was directed by the authority of our Spirit Father. That's what makes it Holy. The writings provide basic instruction for the alignment of mankind's body, soul, and spirit.

The writers of the Bible eventually died, but their documents have endured time. The Scriptures are "Living Words" that are eternal. Even if the books are destroyed, the Word is still alive in the spirit realm and can be rewritten by humans at any time. The "Living Word" is energy coming from the spirit realm and it cannot be destroyed. It is infinite, meaning it is endless in time. Some things are simply beyond our human understanding.

Allow me to explain this concept another way. We can only talk about dimensions of diversity from a physical perspective – age, race, ethnicity, gender, disabilities, skin color, religion, sexual orientation, etc. That's because our way of thinking is influenced by what we see, feel, touch, hear, and taste. Emotions influence the mind, while the brain tells the body what to do. There's human evidence that confirms what the Old and New Testaments tell us is Truth.

I wasn't always conscious that my body is not the real me. But what I realized as a young child is that I was never alone. My first encounter with the spirit realm occurred when I was six years old. I shared a room with my two brothers. One day my curiosity got the best of me, and I told my older brother to pull his pants down so I could see his "weenie." Next thing I knew I was banished to the attic to spend five years in a space that was more like a closet than a room.

This was the only empty space available in our boarding house. The other rooms were occupied by two cousins and two other adults who provided my parents with income. Without understanding that my parents had a mortgage to pay, my six-year-old mind assumed I was being punished for my "sin." No one told me otherwise.

Climbing two flights of stairs through the dark of night was terrifying. My older brother would hide under the stairs and say, "boooo!" My cousins would pull the drapes closed to keep the heat in their room and the coldness of winter in mine. The only assurance I had was the love of a Spirit Father who shared a very private area of my life. He was my companion every night when I climbed that dark mountain. He was the comforter who sent my dog to the attic during those cold winter nights to keep me warm. It was this unconditional love that kept me from losing my sanity.

Forgiveness wasn't a word in my vocabulary. I was beyond angry. My brothers had a nice warm room off the kitchen, and I was confined to a closet in the attic. By the time I was age eight, I was totally convinced I had been adopted. My relationship with my mother was horrific. I wasn't just angry; I was determined to get even! Whenever I entered a room, a problem came with me.

Over the next few years my bad attitude and bad behavior continued to deteriorate. I wanted out of the attic. To "save" my soul, my mother decided to send me to church. I had just turned ten and that's where I learned what it means to be a "hypocrite."

I quickly decided that the church is full of people who believe one thing on Sunday and then do the opposite the rest of the week. My human father was one of them. Every Sunday My mother called him a "hypocrite." She didn't like church, so she sent my brothers and I with my father. On Friday and Saturday, he played cards and overindulged in alcohol with his friends, and every Sunday he faithfully went to church to repent.

I discovered early on that a church building is not the only source of spiritual power. For over a year I had been preparing for this ritual exercise called "Holy Confirmation." To prove you're a Christian, a believer is expected to make a public affirmation of their faith, recommit themselves to the responsibilities of their baptism, and receive laying on of hands by a Bishop. I assumed this was supposed to stop me from being an impossible child; to make me a godly person. I had absolutely no understanding of this ritual. Four years in the attic had turned me into a monster. I was a ten-year-old with an exorcist for a mother who was determined to "drive the devil out of me."

My next encounter with the spirit realm actually happened during the "Confirmation" ceremony. I have a learning disability, a processing disorder, so the catechism classes were extremely confusing. I had a difficult time staying focused. Frankly, I wasn't interested in learning something that I couldn't comprehend. What I did understand was the consequence if I didn't pass the class. My mother would surely kill me. So, I prayed for help. I had no idea how I was going to get through that little black book called *The Book of Common Prayer*, much less make a public affirmation of faith. I needed my Spirit Father and he was right on time.

The teacher's name was Miss Polité. She was the first known appearance of "Miss Piggy" before the Muppets were even created.

For sure my brother and I were going to hell for calling her that. But through her lessons, I became fascinated with the concept of "Living Words." *How can this be possible?* At the time I didn't understand that learning occurs when the spirit of mankind is awakened to something. I questioned everything. *Why were Adam and Eve created perfect? What was the sense if God knew they would sin?*

Thanks to Miss Polite I learned there's a process that happens in the heart, not in the mind. If nothing else, her Confirmation classes helped me understand the act of creation. As a child I was always using my imagination in a meaningful way. I created potholders for my mother using a loom. I created a fan for my father using popsicle sticks. There was always a sense of satisfaction when I created something for someone else. In fact, I could feel the love flow when I presented these gifts. Although I was a child, I realized that all of us are born with a purpose to create something good for humanity.

In obedience to the church and to "God," I memorized the catechism to keep my mother from beating the hell out of me. Did I understand what I was doing? No! But I knew I loved the Lord.

My mother had bought me a beautiful white dress with a matching white veil for the occasion. It made me feel "holy," like something extraordinary was going to happen. To this day I don't remember very much about the ceremony itself, other than kneeling at the altar. What I do remember is the Bishop laying his hands on my head and praying for the Holy Spirit to come. Suddenly I was engulfed in a blanket of something so wonderful, so comforting, so unforgettably peaceful. I imagined I was an angel. In an instant I felt released from my fear of darkness; fear of climbing to a dark attic.

With the Bishop's hands still on my head, I saw a flash of light and immediately fainted. Down to the floor I went in that beautiful white dress thinking: *Oh, Jesus, my mother is going to kill me!*

When I came back from wherever I went during my blackout, the only thing I could remember was that feeling of peace followed by a flash of light. I honestly thought I had died and gone to heaven.

How I got from kneeling at the altar to sitting in a chair in the church office I will never know. Obviously, someone carried me. I was grasping for breath from the scent of ammonia in my noise. A hand was pushing smelling salt in my face. I pushed it away and thought: *Are you crazy? I can't breathe!*

Only when the Bishop smiled and touched my cheek did I know I was still alive; everything was going to be okay. When he asked what happened, I told him that I had gone into the light. My parents didn't realize what that meant, but the Bishop knew. During my Confirmation ceremony I had an encounter with the spirit realm. I was never afraid of the dark again. My Spirit Father had created me to have a gentle spirit, to be quick to love, and slow to anger. And that's exactly how I am today, 68 years later.

Don't get me wrong. I didn't suddenly become a saint. I was still living in the attic with emotions controlling my actions. As a child, I didn't have knowledge that mankind is born of the spirit and our spirit lives *in* our body. I learned this later after years of ups and downs and disappointments. So don't think I magically turned into a bible-reading ten-year-old. My anger and aggressive behavior didn't suddenly disappear with that spiritual encounter.

It took years to become what my Spiritual Father created me to be – loving and peaceful. My soul and spirit were weak, and my actions came from worldly thinking. I was a child with a grudge. Over time, negative thoughts became bad habits and consequences resulted from my own bad behavior. What was happening to me was not good and I knew it. My parents were nice people who were stuck with a difficult child.

Every night I would go to my "special space" in the attic, get on my knees, and ask my Spirit Father to fix my life. I wanted my parents to love me, especially my mother. I wanted out of that attic.

When we experience the world with a connection to the spirit realm our path in life is greatly influenced by our Spirit Father. Don't misunderstand this: As children we live according to the way we see the world from a human perspective. I was banished to the attic, away from the family. In my young mind, I was placed in this dark dungeon because I sinned; I asked my brother to pull down his pants. My childhood attitude and behaviors were guided by extreme anger toward my parents. *How could they do this to me?* My behavior was also a response to my emotions. *I'm very, very angry!*

I saw the attic as punishment; my parents saw the mortgage. They were struggling to keep our house. I was struggling to keep my sanity. Years later I became aware of the differences in our perceptions. My parents had to choose between the attic or the basement. Of course, I would have been angry with either choice.

Some 25 years later, when my father became ill, I felt obligated to help my mother. I left a lucrative career in New York and moved to another state where I spent the next 27 years caring for my aging parents. There's no way to express the pure joy that resulted from that decision. Let me share with you what I eventually learned.

Unconditional love is more than just a warm, peaceful feeling you get sitting in church singing or listening to a good sermon. After some intense soul-searching, the spirit seeks a purpose that goes far beyond just eating, sleeping, working, and playing. That truly is the life of an animal. But with a focus on doing good, the soul, which is connected to the spirit, can visualize a world that is void of greed, immorality, selfishness, and physical temptations. That's spiritual maturity. That's living life more abundantly.

The awakening of the soul to *Truth* is an "ah-ha" moment that comes from within. The whole person becomes the creator of a higher order of thinking, empowered with emotional intelligence to follow the direction of his or her spirit. Free will is no longer self-centered but is guided by the "Living Words" that come from a deeply rooted spirit center of unconditional love. There's a desire to build better relationships with people you care about.

The point is this: change will never happen on its own. As human beings with nothing but a body, we have no power. But an individual with a heart for change can ask our Spirit Father for help. That might sound crazy, but it's true. How do I know? I have matured enough to where I can recognize Truth that has existed before time began. I believe that Scripture was written by men inspired to fulfill their purpose and share Truth with the world.

Now the question becomes: Can YOU accept the "Living Words" in the Bible to be Truth? Before you answer that question, keep reading. Hopefully, you will understand how a connection with your Spirit Father can make a difference to better your life.

I am speaking in human terms because that's all I know. But as you continue to read, make the choice to keep an open mind. Don't get caught up in religious controversy. I don't know any believer today who's human body has been alive for 2,700 years. That's the age of the text in the Bible. Keep in mind the "Living Word" isn't speaking to your humanity, it's talking to your spirit.

Here's the point: We make decisions almost every minute of our life. Some are important, and some are not so important. Suppose you decide to buy a luxury car that you can't really afford and then you lose your job. Think about how you would react. What kind of behavior and attitude would you display?

Your success in life depends on your ability to think problems through and make wise decisions. If you make the wrong choices, your reactions can create even more problems. Here's an example.

Imagine you and your boss are having a conversation about why he fired you. There are always two sides to every story; two different ways to look at any situation. Here's one way to respond.

Boss: *I'm sorry to have to lay people off, especially people like you, who have worked so hard.*

You: *What! You can't do this to me! I just bought a new car! I have a big car payment!*

Boss: *If things get better, I will try to bring you back.*

You: *You fired me! What makes you think I'd ever work for you again!*

A world perspective views everything from the material side, often creating anger and anxiety. You just lost your job and now you don't know how you will make the next car payment. Your attitude and reaction are sparked by your emotions, which created conflict. The situation could even escalate to something worse.

The decisions we make and the actions we take are not always the right choices, especially when they are based on emotions rather than reasoning.

Now, what if you spoke from the heart? Your boss is trying to save his business. Imagine what would happen if your response were guided by a Spirit Father who is infinitely wiser, more loving, more generous, kinder, and more forgiving than any human being could possibly ever be.

Suppose you wanted to keep your job. Let's look at the same situation from a more balanced perspective. You and your Boss are having a conversation about the survival of his struggling business. A more compassionate, wiser response from you might go like this:

Boss: *The Company is in trouble. I'm sorry, but I have to lay people off, including a hard worker like you.*

You: *Oh, wow! I just bought a new car! Is there anything I can do to help?*

Boss: *I'd hate to lose you. But I just can't afford to pay a big salary right now.*

You: *Look, why don't I take a pay cut until things get better. I really like working for you.*

Boss: *Wow! If you'd do that I promise I will make it up to you. Let's consider it an investment.*

You don't have to accept whatever life brings your way. A response based on logic and reason can produce different results. This doesn't mean you will *always* get what we want. Rarely do people get everything they want. The key is to negotiate. Start with a foundation of mutual respect that can result in a win-win for all.

There's a correlation between relationships you've formed and what has happened in your life so far. This is what you need to know about yourself. Relationships can move you forward or set you back. Attitude can make all the difference in how you get along with other people. So, let's dig deeper to see the impact of the two most important relationships in your life – family and friends. You can rarely choose the people who come into your life, but you can choose how you deal with them.

As young children, we experienced dealing with different kinds of people in different circumstances. Some connections formed along the way were very good, while others might not have been so great. It may be very uncomfortable to think about it, but every interaction you had with people during your early childhood either moved you forward or pushed you back; either built you up or put you down.

I am talking about the years between birth and age eight, when children learn more quickly than any other time in life. Perhaps you had a sibling that was a bully; or your mother smothered you by refusing to let you be more independent. Are you ready to stretch your comfort zone?

Explain a childhood experience when you felt insecure?

_____

_____

_____

_____

How did you react to this situation?

_____

_____

_____

Quite often there are family members who make us feel as if our lives are being lived just for them, especially parents and siblings. As time goes by, we believe that's just the way things are supposed to be and there's nothing we can do about it. After all, as children, we are not the ones in charge.

Explain what it's like to be a member of your family.

If you pause and think seriously about the people who impacted your life as a child, you can better understand how these human interactions had a positive or negative impact on the attitude and behavior you display today.

Looking at the past with new eyes I can remember being a rebellious teenager. I saw myself as a "nerd" and wanted to be "cool" like the other girls my age. I wanted desperately to "belong." This had a strong effect on my self-image and self-confidence. Bad decisions in my personal life kept dragging me down.

Having grown up with three brothers and no sisters, I was a "tomboy" at heart. I could hit and throw a ball further than any boy on the block. In truth, I preferred having male friends. Boys valued my athletic ability, while girls were bullies who constantly teased me. I didn't want to be a boy, but I felt left out as a girl. What's worse, no one understood or even cared about how I felt.

I liked hanging out with guys and engaging in games that were physical. Feeling awkward and uncomfortable around females became a part of my personality. I just didn't fit in. I'm certain growing up a tomboy worried my parents, but I didn't care. For me, sports were far more important than academics. I felt more comfortable in jeans than I did wearing a dress.

As a teenager, all the women I was exposed to were miserable stay-at-home moms, including my own mother. For me, there was nothing exciting about being born a female.

Back then, boys were expected to go to college and girls were expected to get married and have children. What a bummer!

By the time I was in high school I had stopped climbing trees and playing football in the mud. Now, I was in a gym playing girls' basketball and co-ed volleyball. And of course, I excelled at sports.

But I was about to be pushed out of school and into an adult world. On the downside, I had a learning disability. I didn't see college in my future. I was going to graduate from high school with no goal, no vision, and no future. I saw trouble ahead. Meanwhile a war was raging in Vietnam War. Families in our neighborhood had lost far too many sons. So, when the U. S. president announced that married men could avoid the draft, I did a friend a favor. Like I said, back then girls were expected to get married, have children and stay at home. Despite the objection of our parents, we got married.

I had just turned eighteen. Little did I know that my husband would be a control freak. He wanted to control every aspect of my life, from deciding where I could work , to taking my paycheck every week, to giving harsh criticism that made me feel worthless. *The friend I married was no longer my friend.*

Looking back, I can see how weak my spirit had become. I was a victim of my own negative thinking. What my husband wanted was not what I wanted. His goal was to have a large family with a stay-at-home wife, like our mothers. Well, I wasn't going for that. My goal was to pursue a career as a writer. And the likelihood of a long-lasting, happy marriage became very slim.

By now you're probably wondering what happened to that young child who was connected to the spirit realm. Scripture says the flesh is weak and that's true. When you constantly hear, "I'm right and you're wrong," you begin to lose your *true* self in the lie. Family and friends make you feel guilty about what you are or are not doing.

I was so out of balance in my relationships that I created a false sense of reality, just to survive. I began to dream about a handsome superhero who would rescue me from a nasty villain. The dreams turned into written stories that I tried to get published, and in writing them I discovered a hidden talent.

I had always wanted to be a writer, but negative thoughts had me convinced it was impossible. Everyone said I needed a college education to succeed. But writing was something that I seemed to do naturally and had always done well. English was my best subject in high school. I also had a vivid imagination.

Thinking about how much I liked to "win" helped me to find a career path as a junior writer. I was surprised when I was offered a job in the advertising industry. And one of the most senior creative directors at a prestigious ad agency offered to mentor me. For me, it was a dream come true.

I couldn't believe my good fortune. It was the opportunity of a lifetime. Except a stumbling block was my husband. He absolutely *"forbid"* me to take a job in New York City. His role for me as a wife and mother didn't include an advertising career.

As mind-boggling as this may seem, I had spent five years living a lie. My marriage was all about rules and property rights and fear. It had little to do with love, which is supposed to be patient, kind and compassionate. Love does not say "you can't" when you know that "you can." Love does not threaten to "divorce" you if you don't do what you are told. It's important for women to recognize the signs of a verbally abusive relationship and do something about it.

My dream of becoming a writer had come to a fork in the road. It was time to make the most important decision of my life. I could choose to believe the lies that had been drilled into my head, or I could step out on faith and listen to the truth that was in my heart.

For years I had been heavily influenced by people who meant well in giving advice. In my heart I knew that I was not responsible for the physical and verbal abuse that was happening.

Somehow, I was awakened to the idea that it was my personal responsibility to take charge. We had gotten married for the wrong reason. Now, the only person who could save me was me. I had to make the most important decision of my life and the right decision was a matter of survival. I was suicidal and more depressed than anyone knew. I didn't get divorced to write; I got divorced to live.

Most people don't realize that a person's mental well-being can be impacted by an abusive relationship. In order to be appreciated, a person has to have self-respect. Why? Because other people treat you based on the image you project of yourself to the world.

I want you to look in the mirror again. Who do you see? Look deep, beyond your image. What do you see that you would like to change? Don't get me wrong. I'm not encouraging anyone to get a separation or a divorce. I simply want to bring awareness to self. There's a lot of negativities in this world system that influence how you value and perceive yourself. Self-respect has a lot to do with everything you say and do in your relationship with others, as well as what they say and do to you. That's a fact!

If you look beyond the image in the mirror and focus on your inner being, give some thought to your opinion of yourself, your self-esteem and self-confidence. Do you see yourself as valuable?

Yes _____   No _____

People who have a negative image of themselves don't have self-respect and they don't get respect from others either. You could be sending out a powerful message that is totally misunderstood. Or maybe when people say you have a "bad attitude" it's because you actually do. Is that the image you want to project? Is that what you want people to think of you? Let's be real. No one wants that.

Everyone wants to believe and feel they have value; that they are a worthwhile human being. Self-respect begins with having a positive self-image. Keep in mind we create our own thoughts, and consequently, we create a self-image that is a reflection of our positive or negative thoughts.

How we see ourselves in the world becomes how we act in the world. Low self-esteem can affect everything you do and say.

Your human nature is not going to change. But you do have the ability to create a new image of *yourself* by changing the way you think and by controlling the way you act and react. You need to stop relying on other people to make you feel good and being disappointed when it doesn't happen. You need to be your own best friend. Keep in mind that you have the power of choice.

What about self-confidence? It's hard to believe in yourself when people around you always have a negative view of things. Months and years of thinking "I can't" can severely damage your critical thinking. You are not a total failure if you make mistakes.

Friends and relatives probably mean well, but it's up to you to be positive and optimistic. Remember, your mind is the control center of your life. My mother always said, "Take **I can't** out of your vocabulary." That doesn't mean you are not going to have negative feelings from time to time. It happens. Your basic human nature is not going to change, so don't expect that of yourself. You're human.

But when you focus on the spirit realm to make wise choices, you tap into a power source to help you analyze difficult situations, especially ones that may have held you in bondage for years.

Look at it this way. There are dimensions to the relationships we form throughout our lives. As children we depend on our parents to supply our basic human needs—like food, clothing, shelter, and our physical and mental well-being. And at some point we grow up.

Unfortunately, far too many adults are mentally lifeless. They grew physically, but never achieved mental maturity. Like children, they are still in the *dependence* stage, still focused on "me" in their relationships. *You have to take care of me.* People in that state of mind rely on others to get what they want—to think for them, to make decisions for them, to provide them with a sense of worth and security. In other words, like dust, they go wherever the wind blows. You probably know some adults like that. They have not moved beyond their childish dependencies. If their basic needs aren't met, they feel empty and incomplete. Their neediness is obvious. It's easy for others to take advantage, to manipulate, to get what they want from these spiritually weak individuals. This is why so many teens join gangs or have babies out of wedlock. They depend on others to make them feel valued. The natural growth process is disrupted.

Most of us fluctuate between dependency and independence. It's not uncommon. People who are independent often see themselves through a self-interest lens. Life is all about "I." *I don't need you; I can do it myself.* The problem with "I" relationships comes when a person is sowing one thing but is expecting to reap something entirely different. You harvest from the seed that was planted.

People focused on "I" often become slaves to self-fulfillment and fear. They are only concerned about "self," while neglecting the "little things" that are so very important to preserving a relationship. They can turn on the charm and practice manipulative techniques to get what they want. But they can't maintain a rewarding, long-term connection with other people.

The saying "what we sow, we will inevitably reap" is Truth. The divorce court is filled with self-centered "I" personalities—people who are so full of love for themselves that they have no room to love anyone else. It's no wonder so many marriages end in divorce.

Quality relationships are tied to the spiritual realm. This type of relationship usually involves people who value principles like trust, honesty, mutual respect, and good communication. They think deeply about what really matters most with their "we" connections. In maintaining quality relationships with others, these people strive to do the right things for the right reasons in the right way.

Truly *interdependent* people mature to a level where they can have a meaningful co-existence with others. They think in terms of "we" and not "me." *We can combine our talents and work as a team.* Truth prompts them to see people as they are and accept them for who they are. It's called unconditional love.

Quality relationships cannot grow out of illusions and lies. The reason why so many of us wind up in relationships that tear us down is because we go for the illusion of "love" instead of long-term development and growth. We make wrong choices and bad decisions based on unrealistic expectations.

The purpose of a relationship is not to have some other person make you feel complete; you are already complete in your spirit. You just don't know it yet.

When two people get into a relationship with the goal of finding themselves, they generally experience just the opposite—they lose themselves. They give up too much of who they *really* are by trying to stay together. This is *not* how our Spiritual Father intends human relationships to be. Trouble comes when one person interjects selfish conditions into the relationship, forcing the other person to prove their love. Human nature tends to misuse what is not appreciated.

Let's be honest. There's no way a relationship can work if we try to fill the role of what someone else wants us to be. Quality relationships are built when the actions and reactions of two people contribute to mutual growth.

Marriage should be an equal opportunity to become one's *true* self, to lift life together to its highest potential as "one flesh." It is a partnership in which one person compliments the other; and where one is weak the other is strong. It doesn't matter who has what skills individually so long as both people benefit from the connection. Sometimes our biggest mistake in a relationship is that we don't show appreciation for those who are important to us.

Tragically, we live in a worldly society where the temptations of money, sex and power are the measuring sticks for success in a relationship. Yet, these elements are often the very things that come between couples and destroy families if they remain unchecked.

In the past, our choices have brought consequences we would rather have lived without…if you know what I mean. We've all been there. Unfortunately, we can't change reality. We can't undo what has already been done. What we can do is recognize the consequences of bad choices and learn from our mistakes. We can make a conscious decision to change.

Of course, change isn't something any of us can do on our own. I mean it's impossible to rely on our own efforts to change our basic human nature. Mankind does not possess this kind of supernatural power. Always remember that the soul depends on the body to have experiences on earth, to learn and grow in alignment with the spirit.

Human power is natural and what is natural is not spiritual. That's Truth! The soul cannot function without the power of the spirit. The lessons we learn in life prepare the true *self* to live in the spirit, so when the body dies the soul and the spirit can live on. Where depends on what the person believes and how he or she has lived.

Fortunately, life is experienced in different stages. That's why the future offers so much hope if the body is alive. I wrote in my book *The People Zoo*, **"It's better to be a live dog than a dead lion."** This is a quote from scripture (Ecclesiastes 9:4) written by Solomon, who is still considered to be the wisest man who ever lived. These two animals represent different types of human personalities.

In ancient times a dog was looked upon as an unclean scavenger, while the lion was a majestic "king of the beast." King Solomon used this comparison as a powerful lesson about life and death.

In death, the high and mighty lion knows nothing, hopes for nothing, and can get nothing. His life on earth has ended. Yet, there is still hope for the lowly dog who is still alive and can change.

Life is a journey filled with mistakes. We learn a little bit more about making the right decisions each time we fall and must pull ourselves back up again. In fact, that's how the soul and the spirit get stronger. When we focus on the spirit realm to make a choice, we tap into our inner ability to analyze a difficult situation, especially one that may have held us in bondage for years. Our Spirit Father is our ultimate helper. This supernatural connection causes the soul to see the world differently; to view our bad relationships differently, and to have a different perspective of *self*. This trait is what we all inherit from our Spirit Father – the ability to know the difference between decisions that serve a good purpose and decisions that lead to unfortunate consequences. There is nothing mysterious about how the inner power of the spirit realm can be activated.

When we come to know ourselves in a deeper, more meaningful way, we tend to interact with others differently—always guided by something greater than our selves. There are specific principles that are fundamental for building a quality relationship—things like love and trust.

Truth grows out of the ability to make and keep commitments, to be caring and responsible, to love unconditionally. Does your Spirit Father want you to have loving, successful relationships? The answer is absolutely! Of course, the key is to build the *right* kind of relationship by creating a spirit connection first. When the soul is in perfect alignment with the spirit, humans have the ability to love unconditionally, and to have thoughts that are good, pure, honest and true. That's what it means to a Spirit Nature.

Through our relationships with others, we experience higher aspects of our true *self*. This is why relationships aligned with the spirit never "fail." They may not produce what we want, but every experience helps us to come into the realization of our *true self*.

Self-awareness is the ability to stand apart from ourselves and closely examine who we really are. You can experience this for yourself. Close your eyes for a moment and imagine yourself as a spiritual being having a human experience. In your mind's eye, what do you "see?"

Explain how you see yourself as a spirit being:

_____

_____

_____

Now describe how you see yourself as a human being:

_____

_____

_____

You can't have healthy relationships with others if you don't know yourself. Think about how you relate to other people. Take the time to self-assess why some of your relationships may not be working. This is not an exercise of self-criticism; it's simply a way to gain self-knowledge for you to better understand *self*. Remember to answer each item honestly so you have a *true* picture.

GET TO KNOW YOURSELF	MOSTLY	SOMETIMES	RARELY
I have a positive attitude about life.			
I'm confident in the decisions I make.			
I recognize bad habits that block my success.			
I feel motivated when I'm working on a job.			
I deal with people honestly and truthfully.			
I have patience with people I don't like.			
I can take constructive criticism.			
I show self-confidence in everything I do.			
People I know trust me.			
I'm sensitive to the needs of others.			
I'm good at managing my time.			
I'm committed to stay on a job I don't like.			
I speak frankly about how I feel.			
I make decisions based on my gut feelings.			
I respect authority and obey rules.			
I get what I want out of my relationships.			
I have good moral principles.			

If you want to improve your relationships, simply work on the one thing over which you have control—your *inner self*. Think for a moment about relationships you value.

Our natural instinct is a sense of wanting to "belong" and be accepted by family members. Describe your relationship with your family.

_____

_____

_____

Decide on one thing you could do that would significantly improve the quality of your relationship with a family member.

_____

_____

_____

There's something deep within humans that desires to belong to the "in" crowd. Because of this inner desire, some people tend to choose the wrong companions. Today's fast-paced lifestyle can hold many traps, especially in a money, sex, and power culture. Describe what you have learned about choosing the wrong friends?

_____

_____

_____

_____

Step Three - Restoration
The Ultimate Human Experience

It's better to start this next step in your personal "My" Space. Remember, your soul and spirit are your inner being. What you think influences your emotions and actions every day. Just like when you exercise your body, it's important to have a healthy soul and a strong spirit.

Your journey is about to take a giant leap. So, let's prepare your mind and body to unite with the spirit realm. To stay focused, take deep breaths to help your body relax and prepare your mind for another awakening. Take a deep breath, hold it for three seconds, and slowly breathe out. Repeat this process a few times. Once you feel relaxed and ready to focus, spend the next *30* minutes reading and seeing your soul being restored through a spiritual lens.

In the last step you completed a self-knowledge exercise. Look back to see how often you checked the "rarely" column. What does this exercise tell you about yourself? It would probably be easier for people who know you best to describe how you react to situations. Rarely do we see ourselves the way others see us. Keep thinking about the relationships you've formed throughout your life as we explore the concept of happiness and contentment.

Most people in modern society interpret happiness as "living the good life." But is that what happiness really means?

Back in 1776, the founders of America considered happiness a natural human right. In fact, the pursuit of happiness is a well-known statement in the Declaration of Independence. Before the revolution, the colonists were under the control of Great Britain. They were not happy. What the Declaration of Independence was saying is that every American citizen has the right to control their own path in life in pursuit of happiness.

As human beings with a creator, Thomas Jefferson believed that we inherit the right to "Life, Liberty, and the pursuit of Happiness" from our Spirit Father. This belief is the basis of American democracy, but the U.S. Constitution, the rule of law in the United States, doesn't include any of these words. Why? Because no one government can guarantee everyone "Life, Liberty, and the pursuit of Happiness."

I'm certain four million slaves held in captivity in America were not happy about their "life and liberty." Picking cotton every day from sunup to sunset isn't exactly the "good life." From a slave's perspective, "happiness" meant the pursuit of wealth for white plantation owners at the expense of other human beings.

Everyone's idea of happiness is not the same. I thought I knew what happiness was when I achieved success as an award-winning writer in the advertising industry. Admittedly, I was a "workaholic," overspending time and money trying to find happiness.

My second marriage lasted 18 years, but my husband obviously wasn't "happy." Our relationship was all about money and the things I could buy him. Climbing the ladder of success and winning awards gave me a sense of achievement, and all the while my husband was trying to find himself. When he left me for another woman, I was devastated. I couldn't understand what made him so unhappy.

The word happiness is most used to describe a feeling of peace and contentment. But in a world of chaos and confusion, there are a lot of things going on to influence the soul. I wasn't happy in the marriage either, but I didn't give up. I honestly believed he would change.

I finally realized that happiness is a choice, and no one has to be held hostage by difficult circumstances. My husband chose to be happy with someone else, and I chose to be happier without him. It's worth noting that money can meet our basic needs, but it can't buy happiness. That was a valuable lesson for me to learn.

What about you? Life in this world has become incredibly toxic. Millions of people are in a continual state of stress, depression, anxiety, bipolar disorder, and other mental illnesses. Some even take "happy pills" to treat these conditions. The truth is no chemical drug can turn someone into a happy person. Human nature doesn't work that way. Restoration of an unhealthy soul is not easy when brokenness overshadows Truth. Substance abuse is nothing more than an artificial escape from reality. No matter how good "happy pills" make a person feel, drugs won't solve their problems. It's only a temporary fix. The question then becomes: *What does living a happier, more fulfilled life mean?*

To answer this question, I had to shift to a higher consciousness of myself. It all comes down to recognizing the key elements of a living soul, which comes from the spirit realm. In the last step we learned that the soul lives in the womb before it is born into the physical world. This means every physical body has a soul.

Bottom line: The human body wants nourishment; it desires to be loved in the physical sense; it wants material things. Yet, there is always an inner emptiness once these desires are fulfilled. When the body serves as an end to itself, then it becomes a substitute rather than a means of personal self-development through a living soul.

Look at it this way. The soul is how the human body experiences life. As long as the human body is alive there is hope to find joy and happiness. Remember what Solomon said: "It's better to be a live dog than a dead lion." As long as there is life, there is hope.

The fact that you are reading this book is proof you are not dead and there's hope you can enjoy life more abundantly in the future. It's also proof that your soul is alive because you can feel, think, and have the freedom to make choices. By now you should understand that *true* happiness comes from within. The soul's control over the body is an automatic thing that is directed by our thoughts. This is why it's critical to understand the role of the soul.

The Ancient Greek philosopher Aristotle was the first person to state that "happiness is the meaning and purpose of life; the whole aim and end of human existence." He proclaimed this idea more than 2,300 years ago. What Aristotle was saying is that behind every human goal and dream is the desire to find peace and happiness.

My daughter recently asked me if I was happy. I had to think deeply about her question. I'm perfectly content with my life. So, I had to ask myself: *What makes me happy?*

I looked back over my life and thought about all the things that contributed to my past misery. In the past, a lack of self-confidence and low self-esteem had limited my potential to be happy. I was like dust, being tossed about whichever way the wind blew. At a time when I should have been my own best friend, I was my greatest enemy. And like most people who are dust, I had a misconception about what the pursuit of happiness meant. My ladder to success was against the wrong wall.

Back then my value system was different. I was an award-winning writer at top advertising agencies, selling people cigarettes, makeup, luxury cars, diamonds. I honestly thought happiness was being able to buy the material things I sold. Let me explain how our Western culture works. It's designed to make poor people buy things they can't afford, and rich people buy things they don't' really need. That's the idea behind America's value system of economic growth. Buy! Buy! Buy! My job was to sell using all types of media, even if the product wasn't good for the consumer.

Values are what make people tick. Our personal values are how each of us sees the world and why we do the things we do. That's the current problem with our democracy and Western civilization. People have become selfish and greedy. Let's be honest, we all need food, clothing, and shelter. But the motive in capitalism is to make a profit – by any means necessary. Meanwhile, the government keeps borrowing from the national treasury to keep the voters happy.

It took years for me to realized that people who are content don't want more than they need. Scripture tells us to be happy with what we have and give to the needy. In Philippians 4:11-12 the Apostle Paul writes: *"I have learned to be content with whatever I have. I know what it is to have little, and I know what it is to have plenty. In any and all circumstances I have learned the secret of being well-fed and of going hungry, of having plenty and of being in need."*

There's a valuable lesson in this message. At the very heart of our soul are values that influence how we feel, how we think, and how we make choices.

Identify Your Core Personal Values

You can never be happy if you don't know your core values. Before going any further, use the exercise below to prioritize what's most important in your life. The path you are going down will make more sense when you prioritize **FIVE** things below that you value **MOST**.

ONLY CIRCLE FIVE THINGS THAT YOU VALUE MOST.

Achievement	Commitment	Fun
Affluence	Community	Fame
Authority	Dignity	Friendship
Amusement	Devotion	Hope
Ambition	Discipline	Honor
Acceptance	Effectiveness	Justice
Comfort	Enthusiasm	Loyalty
Compassion	Excitement	Power
Competition	Equality	Wealth
Credibility	Entertainment	Winning
Challenge	Empathy	Work
Control	Family	Security
Contentment	Faith	Structure
Confidence	Fitness	Self-reliance
Connection	Freedom	Success

Now add **four** Values from the list above that you value **LEAST**.

1. _____

2. _____

3. _____

4. _____

Every human needs a personal value system. Some common characteristics already existed within us before we were conceived. Remember, we are a soul living in a human body. Qualities like compassion, love, and morality are unique traits that were given to us during our spiritual creation. Thank you, Abba (Father).

Scientists believe that each human being is thrust into the world with the innate sense to know the difference between right and wrong. This doesn't necessarily mean everyone is always going to have good thoughts. We have all strayed from spiritual principles once the mind became influenced by a worldly system.

Let's review the key elements of the soul again. Keep in mind these three elements are interconnected.

Emotions react to the physical body's five senses. It's how we come to feel about a situation and are influenced by our feelings.

Mind is where thoughts develop and grow as the brain responds to experiences and the physical situations we encounter.

Free Will is where the Mind and Emotions interact within the Soul to make a choice on what action the body should take in response to a situation or circumstance.

What every human being needs to understand is that the most valuable quality inherited from our Spirit Father is the ability to have a higher order of awareness of *self*. We are all different in one way or another on the outside, yet we are all created the same on the inside – with a living soul and a living spirit.

Speaking of the soul: as important as having a personal value system is the ability to control your Emotions. Your human body doesn't have the ability to do this on its own. The human body reacts to every impulse that you feel. If you want a life of true misery all you have to do is let your emotions be in control of your soul.

You're probably asking yourself: *"What does the soul have to do with happiness and misery?"* EVERYTHING! Whether or not you realize it, attitudes and behaviors are developed in the soul. It takes self-awareness to create a mind-set that can control what you say and how you react. Self-awareness begins with acknowledging that you are a spirit with a living soul embedded in a human body. If you have a strong, healthy soul, what follows is mental well-being. Keep in mind that happiness is the opposite of misery. You can't have both elements occupying the same space at the same time.

For me, the discovery of how the soul works is what changed my life. Many times, over the years, I have made far too many bad decisions and suffered the consequences. In business; in money matters, in relationships, and in raising my kids. One day I had an "ah-ha" moment during my chaotic life. I was in church, a place that always made me feel good in the time of storms. The choir was singing a song called, "It is well with my soul" and I was singing along. That was far from the truth.

Tears started running down my cheeks. I was singing a song that did not reflect my emotional state. It was not well with my soul. I will never forget the experience of realizing that negative thoughts were being created out of my own unhappiness and discontent. It was a revelation. A little voice inside me was saying: *"Problems can't be solved with emotions alone. You need to wake up, girl! Restore your soul!"*

Afterwards, I had this deep desire to explore a spiritual path that would eventually lead me to intentional living. If things were going to change, I had to be more proactive and explore the workings of my soul – my thoughts, feelings, and free will. It didn't take long to figure out these three key elements were out of alignment in my life. I had to get my house in order. *I deserved to be happy!*

My soul was in desperate need of spiritual therapy. I finally realized that restoration starts and ends with me making a choice. This was yet another "ah-ha" moment. When the mind comes up with solutions, then the will has to decide which path to take. I couldn't have it both ways. One path would lead to a mindset of contentment, while the other would keep me in a life of conflict and confusion. It was a revelation designed to challenge me. Whatever happens in the mind becomes reality in the physical world. Hence, we reap what we sow. In other words, if we plant a bad seed the result will be a bad harvest. That's just how nature works.

One thing that became very clear is that human responses are formed from bad habits. Take body language, for example. My granddaughter tells people how she feels by the way she rolls her eyes, twists her mouth, and shrugs her shoulders. She knows better than to act out what she's thinking with Grandma. I'm old school.

In choosing to communicate with nonverbal body language, a bad attitude can interfere with every relationship a person attempts to make. I recognized this as an emotional flaw that probably carried over from my granddaughter's childhood. But a nasty attitude is not how people see themselves at all. What my granddaughter and others like her don't understand is how much they are limiting their ability to have a better life by not governing their human nature. This is why knowing yourself is so important.

Breaking bad habits is not an easy task, especially for young people who can't handle constructive criticism or accept authority. Unfortunately, accepting responsibility is not one of the traits in my granddaughter's value system. Her generation is one of the reasons I decided to write this book.

Emotional maturity and negative behavior are part of a vicious cycle. If an individual is not able to accept and deal with bad circumstances as a part of life, the results can be poor decisions that have unfortunate consequences. In fact, we're going to deal with emotional intelligence in the next step, because there's a lot more to this topic than just self-control.

Dring my time of restoration, I was reminded that self-awareness is what separates humans from animals. As spiritual beings, we have awareness of our internal and external existence. This is why we can connect with our "Father" in the spirit realm.

How many times have you heard people cry, "Help me God!" Calling out to our Spirit Father is a natural, intuitive action just like calling out for "Mama" when we need something. You have the ability to connect with your Spirit Father and your spirit connects with your soul to provide insight on how to act. Decisions and actions are made with logic and reasoning in the brain, rather than a response to emotions. Animals can't do this, even though they can think. They don't have the ability to reason before making decisions.

Scientific studies of animal behavior have repeatedly revealed that animals react to their five senses. They respond to taste, smell, touch, sight, and hearing. Because of our animal nature, we humans react to our five senses as well. We tend to relate to things we encounter by responding instinctively. As humans, we have no natural power over temptations of the body. The flesh naturally lusts after what it sees, always seeking self-gratification. Scripture calls this "sin," which simply means there's a separation of the soul from the spirit realm.

I'll say it again: humans are created with a natural ability to reason; to think beyond our five senses and our emotions. This is a unique endowment from our Spirit Father. He gives mankind the ability to have independent will; to choose how to respond to any situation.

In life, no act is more supernatural than when a human being can overcome the temptations of their flesh nature and yield to the will of their spirit nature.

We can't control what someone else may do to us. But we can control how we respond if acted upon. Self-control means knowing how to act and when to act. This is the key to restoration of the soul and the happiness that follows. Having a soul simply means you are free in any situation or circumstance to make decisions based on critical thinking, problem-solving, and what you value as important.

In Genesis 1:26, scripture tells us that **"mankind has dominion over the animals."** The superior role of humans over living things is intentional. It's a gift. Our Spirit Father instructs us to care for the earth. Plants and animals must follow a natural order of creation. As spiritual beings having human experiences, we have the option to create our own destiny. What is happening with climate change is an prime example of this control. Mankind is still messing up the environment, despite warning signs from nature. What do you think is going to happen to humans as a result of all the bad seeds that are being planted all over the earth, in the oceans and in the atmosphere? Pollution, global warming, food shortage, warfare...

What does this tell you about choices we've been making so far? Keep in mind human decisions have always been influenced by our personal value systems. Any bad choices our leaders have made will result in consequences you probably don't want to discuss. That's okay. Humans make mistakes. The question is what have we learned from these mistakes? Restoration means forgiveness for all the pain we've caused, even if it means forgiving ourselves.

If you don't deal with the reality of consequences and take responsibility for your decisions, bad situations will continue to happen. You will continue to feel victimized by situations you may or may not have created.

There is a message for you in a poem called *A Dream Deferred*, written by Langston Hughes. He asks: *What happens to a dream deferred?* Although the poem leaves it up to the reader to decide what action to take, the options are very explicit.

> *Does it dry up like a raisin in the sun;*
>
> *Or fester like a sore and run?*
>
> *Does it stink like rotten meat?*
>
> *Or crust and sugar over – like a syrupy sweet?*
>
> *Maybe it sags like a heavy load?*
>
> *Or does it explode?*

Perhaps the most important insight to gain from this poem is to understand your state of emotional well-being at this very moment. I'm not talking about what happened to you in the past that caused you pain; but how you feel about yourself in the present, the here and now. Most of us tend to think we're okay, but the reality is that our life is a mess. In which case, you will need more self-awareness of inner strength to restore your soul. Real change occurs on the inside and evidence of change is reflected in the world.

But first, the soul must deal with unfinished business. Habits don't change on their own. There's no quick fix for bad choices you've already made. Undoubtedly, there will be times when you might feel overwhelmed. We all would rather live without the consequences of bad decisions; but stuff happens. The issue is with how we react to situations and deal with reality. It's not what happens to us that causes pain, but how we respond and learn from our experiences.

Freedom of choice is what causes people to be depressed, anxious, angry, withdrawn, suicidal, and self-destructive. Problems happen in the soul before they become reality. Almost unconsciously, human nature responds to situations that the soul can have control over.

Our normal mental reaction is to view a situation as a problem. We don't realize that the mind is in control of any situation. If the emotions kick in without the brain taking charge, the body reacts to feelings. The trick is to avoid reacting with emotions alone. Humans were created to benefit from having a soul. There will always be a gap between your emotions and your mind. Your body will always respond to feelings, rather than using your gift of reasoning.

Self-knowledge can lead to an alignment of your mind, body, and spirit. With knowledge of how your soul operates, you can analyze a situation with your brain and control your feelings while deciding how to respond. I know this sounds crazy, but your spirit can tell your soul what to do. Try it

Critical thinking involves two very basic skills: problem-solving and decisions-making. The brain is a gift from your Spirit Father and like most people, you probably take it for granted.

In our brokenness the soul is weakened, and the mind is focused on doubt and other negative thoughts. Did it ever occur to you that everything happens in your mind first? In many philosophical theories and religious beliefs, the soul identifies who a person really is. It refers to an inner life with relation to our experiences in the world: our thoughts, emotions, personality, and ability to choose in every situation. This is why success in life depends on the ability to have a strong soul; to think problems through and then make wise decisions. But first and foremost, you must understand your *self*.

Believe it or not, misery is a choice. The response to situations happens in the soul. To be free from misery requires using another gift from your Spirit Father called "free will." In life, bad things are going to happen. Sure, you can decide to take happy pills, but you can't decide what happens if your body becomes dependent on them. There are consequences for every bad decision we make. The good news is that you can change your future by strengthening your soul. You don't have to be stuck in bad situations or circumstances.

Happiness is not decided by the endless things you want, nor is it something you can pursue physically. Brokenness to the point of self-rejection isn't a condition that can be cured with the body alone. The key to happiness is to restore the soul by filling it with the spirit.

 When you look at this picture, what do you see? Is the glass half empty or is it half full? Knowing the details of this 12-ounce glass and its content is very important. Remember in Step One we learned that every substance is made from matter. Look again. Now, think about what you don't see in the glass?

From my own perspective, I see the glass as half full because I'm an optimist. The glass still has the potential to be filled with more liquid. In reality, the glass is already full. While half of the glass contains liquid, the rest of the glass is full of air. This means the glass was never empty. It's what we **don't** see that is more powerful than anything we can ever imagine. Filling the glass will become someone's purpose.

Research suggests that people who see the glass as half full are happier. Of course, that's a subjective opinion because happiness itself is subjective. What we envision all depends on what we value. I personally believe that hope is the key to happiness while on this journey we call life. Hope is the trait I value most because it helps me to have a positive outlook for the future. It keeps me going.

I wake up to sunshine every morning even if it's raining. I smile because the flowers need water to bloom. I don't ignore problems; I simply face them with the hope that there will be a good outcome. From the little that I know of the spirit realm, my hope and expectation is in the sunshine of unlimited tomorrows.

Everyone has the human ability to imagine a better future for themselves. The change that occurs within us is the work of our Spirit Father, the parent who is always with us and never leaves us. Human power is not spiritual power. What is natural is not spiritual. Self-knowledge of this difference is the key to recognizing your own limitations. As human beings, we don't have the power to self-transform. To be "changed" is a blessing from the spirit realm.

By now you should realize that your Spirit Father can help you accomplish more in life than you could ever do on your own. To become a "whole" person, you need to probe the inner depths of your *self* and make a choice to change from the inside out. And then you can take the initiative to make restoration happen! Here's an exercise to get you started.

In the space below, explain how you see yourself in the future:

_____

_____

_____

Write a dream or goal you have that will improve your life?

_____

_____

Sometimes the pressure of the day causes us to behave in a certain way to survive. In fact, some of us feel our absolute worst on the inside because of the way we act and react to the physical world.

Choose at least three behaviors you want to change as you go about your daily activities:

1. _____

2. _____

3. _____

Restoration means letting go of the old and replacing it with something new. The way to find inner peace is to forgive yourself for wrong-doings and take responsibility for what you've done.

- Accept that you are not perfect and that everyone makes mistakes. You can't undo what's already done.

- Admit your mistakes. Think about what you could have done differently. Think about what you learned from your mistakes.

- Restore any damaged relationships. If your actions caused an impact, then someone may be trying to heal because of damage you caused. Show more compassion. How can you repair the harm?

- Let go of painful memories. Whatever happened in the past is in the past. If you can't fix it, leave it there. Accept that you can't do anything about it, and let it go. Don't bring it into your present if you want a better future.

- Don't take the talent and skills you have for granted. They are gifts from your Spirit Father. Use them wisely!

Hopeless people are like gerbils in a cage. They have no direction, no goals, and no positive self-image. A person with low self-esteem never sees or accepts what is considered good. They are confused and feel that no one understands them.

What Do Other People Say About You?

Sometimes we must take a closer look at our own actions to become aware of why we have so much trouble fitting into society. You might also want friends and relatives to go over the list and tell you about yourself. Sometimes other people see what's going on better than we do. They get to watch from the outside. Place a checkmark next to each negative behavior you think is holding your back. Then decide what to do about it.

☐ Always Late	☐ Drug User	☐ Procrastinator
☐ Inconsiderate	☐ Disrespectful	☐ No Ethics
☐ Too Emotional	☐ Insensitive	☐ No Goals
☐ Impulsive	☐ Indecisive	☐ Wastes Time
☐ No Self-Esteem	☐ Uncooperative	☐ Unappreciative
☐ Overuses Slang	☐ Steals	☐ Overspends
☐ Not Courteous	☐ Uncommitted	☐ Know-It-All
☐ Gossiper	☐ Foul Mouth	☐ Breaks Promises
☐ Refuses Advice	☐ Freeloader	☐ Overly Critical
☐ Melodramatic	☐ Picks Fights	☐ Always Dirty
☐ Unsafe Sex	☐ Undisciplined	☐ Selfish
☐ Not Dependable	☐ Compulsive Liar	

You're probably feeling a wide range of emotions right now. I can relate. There was a time when I checked a lot of these behaviors too. I was on a fast track going nowhere. If you are not getting ahead in life, maybe you need to think deeply about what other people see in you. Maybe you need to rethink your fundamental values and consider restoring your soul. Perhaps you need a guide, so you won't be on this journey alone. Don't stop now. Help is on the way!

Step Four - Reaction
The Miracle of Self-Control

The mind is an amazing gift from our Spirit Father. As an element of the soul, the mind is wired to focus on love in the highest possible sense of creation. Because humans exist in a physical body, our thoughts and feelings are directed to life experiences as they happen. Therefore, the mind only focuses on what it knows.

With this step we're going to explore two different paths humans face when dealing with the conscious and the subconscious. We'll go beyond what you've already seen and done to see how your mind has aligned with your emotions and your will. Let's start by taking deep breaths to relax your body and awaken your soul. Breathe in, hold your breath for three seconds and then release it. Repeat this breathing exercise three more times. Once you feel relaxed, let's spend time learning more about your soul.

In the last step you completed an exercise that identified behaviors you believe are holding you back. Take a few moments to review these negative behaviors. What did you learn about your personal character? This exercise revealed habits, both good and bad, that are in your subconscious mind. Bad habits are the ones that keep you from pursuing your dreams.

The brain is like a personal computer. It has two compartments called the subconscious and the conscious. The subconscious mind stores information permanently, including bad habits. We're not aware of this data collection process because it is a function of human nature, like your heart beating to pump blood. It just does it. Everything our human body has ever experienced in the world is stored in our subconscious mind. This is a function of human creation, and nothing can stop the mind from memorizing things unless the brain itself is damaged.

Like a computer, the brain doesn't know the difference between what's right and wrong, it just accepts it. It's important to note that our subconscious mind accepts and stores whatever we experience. Good and bad habits are stored in the subconscious mind.

When we attempt to improve behavior by changing bad habits, the subconscious mind takes over. It's not accustomed to change. What happens next is a combination of fear, doubt, anxiety, and depression that comes forth into the conscious mind. We become conscious of these emotions and act upon them. To feel better, people smoke cigarettes. They drink alcohol or take drugs. These habits have become significant areas of scientific inquiry. Over time the body and brain become used to being satisfied by pacifiers that make the body feel good. The mind has a sense of peace that is a false reality.

The mind uses the brain to control consciousness of ongoing experiences, which in turn influences behavior. We become what we think. But there's a big difference between awareness that happens in the conscious mind versus experiences collected and stored in the subconscious mind. You can't begin to change bad habits unless you know where those habits reside and how they are controlled.

We've already established that the mind is part of the soul. We know the soul exists because it operates in the human body. We also established that it's through the soul that the body experiences life.

It's common knowledge that the mind operates in the brain, which in itself is a very complex organ. Science has discovered that decisions are made deep in the subconscious part of the brain before the conscious is aware. What this means is the mind has two levels of existence that influence our thought and behavior patterns.

Everything living is endowed with a consciousness. Flowers bloom. Birds fly. Animals play. Fish swim. In terms of human consciousness, our awareness is not a mystery. It's the ability to know that we are different than everything else in creation. It's the awareness of knowing where you are right now reading this book, and I am somewhere else communication with you through words.

Everything in creation exists on a different level of consciousness. Mankind is endowed with a higher order of thinking that allows us to have an inner and outer existence as we experience the world.

Self is your being as a whole, your mind, body, and spirit. You are more than the physical presence seen in a mirror. Everything about your self is constantly changing. Aren't you much different now than you were at the age of five or six? You don't look the same; you don't think the same, and you certainly don't act the same. As we go deeper into awareness, you'll see how the mind resides in the soul.

Imagine you've never turned on a light switch. When you do it for the first time, nothing happens. You're in the dark. You have no idea what's wrong because it's a new experience. You immediately become anxious because you don't know what to do. Your emotions are in control of your body, and the darkness freaks you out. You fear what you don't know. You need a drink. You need to vape. You need anything that will make you feel better; to make you feel safe.

But what if? What if this experience has happened before? You flick a light switch, and nothing happens. What if a solution to the problem is stored in your subconscious mind. The only reason you can make an intentional decision deep in your subconscious is because the soul remembers things that have happened in the past. The subconscious mind knows what to do. This memory is brought to the conscious part of the brain. You can reason that the light bulb needs to be changed or the switch needs to be fixed. Your conscious mind can manage your emotions, so your body doesn't need a pacifier. Your conscious mind says you are in control.

Once you are aware of the solution, the conscious mind sends a signal to the brain that the body needs to change the light bulb. But awareness of the problem doesn't necessarily mean the solution will be acted upon. Remember, the soul also has freedom to make choices. In fact, the soul is constantly influenced by bad and lazy habits stored in the subconscious mind. You're not afraid of the dark, so your lazy self decides not to change the light bulb. You turn on the television instead. People choose their reactions.

Free will is what determines whether the light switch will do what it was designed to do — turn on the light. Free will requires action and humans don't always decide to do the right thing.

The privilege of choosing freely from different options is endowed in every human being. The soul experiences what science cannot explain. There's a sense of oneness with the mind, emotions, and freedom to make a choice that is influenced by biases, reasoning and memories. We naturally react to situations and circumstances, freeing emotions so they can be experienced. Unfortunately, our emotions and bad habits stored in the subconscious mind can work against us, causing us to make fast, irrational choices.

All human actions are motivated at the deepest level of our being. Every human thought, every action, every interaction, and every choice is triggered by the mind, emotions, and free will.

In short, the mind is primary, but emotions and free can govern how it functions. For self to be genuinely happy in the world, it's not only necessary to know how the human mind works, but also recognize the authority under which it functions.

The ability to manage our thoughts; to respond by controlling our emotions, and to use common sense when making choices all occur in the soul. Happiness can never be self-generated when we take into consideration the function of the soul. True freedom comes from within. Essentially, it's how we see ourselves that determines choices.

We are made and unmade by our thoughts. The highest level of our human existence is Love and the lowest level is Fear, the ultimate opposite. Scripture tells us that Love overcomes all Fear.

Worldly situations like hunger, climate change, and war generate fear in the subconscious mind. We are living in a time of Fear that most people have never experienced before, especially Americans. The pandemic made things worse because people weren't rational.

How we allow our emotions to affect us is what rules the outcome. Our actions can be a by-product of either love or fear. To change the outcome, we must change the way we think.

In the space below, name three things that you fear most:

1. _____

2. _____

3. _____

Emotion is part of the soul that determines how we feel. There are only two primary emotions – Love and Fear. This is reality. Love produces positive feelings like joy, happiness, peace, contentment, and security. Fear provokes anger, anxiety, depression, and stress. The opposite of Fear is Love. It's impossible for these two emotions to operate in the soul at the same time. The soul must decide to be in one space or the other. Let's explore this Truth for a moment using a recent example of an emotional response.

Fear of suffering and dying is an outcome of the COVID-19 pandemic. Everyone was aware of the deadly disease and feelings of vulnerability were stored in the subconscious mind. People also recalled how Black Americans were victims of 40 years of human experimentation of vaccines conducted at Tuskegee University between 1932 and 1972. The memory triggered fear of the COVID-19 vaccine. Millions of people were suddenly making irrational decisions. They refused to protect themselves by getting vaccinated, wearing masks, or social distancing. As a result, countless citizens across the U.S. and around the world were infected, suffered and died.

Strange as it may seem, most people would rather be confined to a life of unreality. Humans would rather live in a world of illusions; to view reality as how we want things to be rather than how they really are. When the subconscious mind and free will choose to ignore conflict, our human nature is to avoid action because we fear failure. We're afraid of what others might think or say. So, we lie to ourselves, day after day, week after week, until the months turn into years. And nothing in our life changes for the better.

No human being can effectively deal with conflict and feelings without a mindset and belief that change occurs from within.

We all come to points along life's journey where we must take action that may be in direct conflict with our subconscious habits. When faced with change, our emotions can put us in a state of confusion if our view of Truth is unrealistic. Think about what happens on a behavioral level when we aren't honest with ourselves.

Have you ever been in a relationship with a needy person? Maybe that's you. "Falling in love" is an illusion that makes us humans feel happy, satisfied and content with troubling situation, like abuse.

Two people meet, they have a romantic encounter, and they think they're in love. But the problem with love on a physical level is that it is confined to the individual. It is conditioned on each partner feeling the same way. Make me happy, and I'll make you happy. Love me, and I'll love you back. This kind of reaction is unrealistic.

Conditional love is an emotion based on need. There is always the fear that the person you love will not give love in return; or the need will not be fulfilled by the other person. Someone is always getting blamed because expectations aren't met.

Genuine love is given without any conditions. It's more than just a feeling of closeness and a desire to care for someone. It's a supernatural emotion at the highest level that is unconditional, selfless, and sacrificial. It exists within our true *self* and fear cannot occupy the same space as unconditional love.

Look at it this way. Hot and cold are total opposites. Just like Love and Fear, they have opposing characteristics. If something is hot, then it can't be cold at the same time. The two can never coexist in the same space. This is reality.

The soul – a combination of emotion, mind, and free will – must decide and choose to be in one space or the other at any given time.

True love is more than an unrealistic romantic encounter or an unfulfilled sexual experience dependent on a partner. Frustration, anxiety, and disappointment in a relationship are essentially a result of unrealistic beliefs and unmet expectations. We expect something in the relationship to be a certain way and when it isn't, we become frustrated. This emotion is an outcome of fear—fear of losing the person we care about; fear that a loved one is going to change.

Hey, let's be honest about beliefs. To expect the passion and emotions experienced at the beginning of a romantic relationship to last forever is unrealistic. We choose the illusion of love rather than face reality that a quality relationship takes a commitment to long-term collaborative growth. True love exists on a higher plane.

This is why so many people move from one relationship to the next, looking to fill the emptiness that occurs when they ultimately fall "out of love." The expectations are unrealistic. So, when things don't turn out like the illusion, negative emotions begin to run rampant. We start to blame the other person for the mess that we rightly own. Conditional love is created internally in the soul and externally in the physical realm. This is not *true* love.

Emotions is reaction that triggers behavior change. It can put us in a state of confusion when our view of Truth is unrealistic. True love accepts a person for who they are, with all their imperfections.

Let's look at another reaction—anger. In itself, anger is an emotion. It can best be described as a survival mechanism; the red flag that cautions us to protect ourselves when fear arises.

Quite often during a conflict, our view of Truth becomes more and more unrealistic. When the subconscious mind fears someone is trying to hurt us, the initial response is to get angry. Our first instinct in response to anger is to attack. Once we step back and become more aware of the situation, the conscious mind may realize the intention wasn't what we thought it was after all. It's how we manage anger and fear that gets us into trouble.

It's important to understand that emotions can affect us only to the extent that the mind and free will react to situations and circumstances. Reactions are not in and of themselves emotional. The problem is most people let emotions rule their mind and their choices. All of us need to take time to listen to our conscience and make wise decisions based upon spiritual principles.

Wisdom can make all the difference in quality-of-life choices. No one can make wise decisions without understanding and discernment. These are gifts from the spirit realm that operate deep within us.

Knowledge means having the ability to get to the bottom of something that is confusing and see it more clearly. Scientists call this ability "reasoning" Nothing else in creation can use logic to dispel confusion except the human brain. As humans, we can seek to understand the other person's point of view, if we choose. What's more, we can discern differences that make people act the way they do. When we see life through another person's eyes, we view problems from different perspectives. An inner voice speaks to our consciousness using logic, saying *don't throw knives or shoot a gun when you're angry.* By knowing right from wrong, we make wiser choices. It's called "common sense."

Scripture says: *"a gentle answer turns away anger, but a harsh word stirs up wrath"* (Proverbs 15:1).

Without the indwelling presence of a spirit, human beings are emotional hostages to the world. Our human nature is to make irrational choices that result in self-imposed punishment. To live wisely, we must continuously push ourselves to gain knowledge, to think rationally about circumstances and situations. And to be completely honest with ourselves when it comes to dealing with inner conflicts. How we react will always determine how well our human body lives in harmony with our inner being.

People often think they need pacifiers to be able to cope with life's difficulties. Drugs and alcohol are temporal. Take time to look back over your life and see where reactions have gotten you.

Some of us understand spiritual principles better than others because we read and study Truth; and we connect with our Spirit Father to apply wisdom to all that we've learned.

Personally, I made a commitment to bring knowledge to others by sharing my life experiences and not simply learning from them.

Here's what I've learned about life. As human beings, we grow spiritually by dealing with conflict. The soul, which is the true self, dwells in the body and experiences life through human actions and reactions. The spirit, which is also the true self, gives strength to the soul. Don't forget you are a spirit having a human experience.

Scripture teaches in Hebrews 1:1-6 that *"faith gives reality to things hoped for and evidence of things not seen."* Faith is the way we tap into the spirit realm and experience a relationship with our Spirit Father. Faith believes in the existence of a Supreme Being, a single deity, and acts on the reality of that Truth. But faith must also be lived through actions to give our human existence meaning and purpose. We must love our Spiritual Father enough to have faith in how he tells us to live on earth as human beings.

Think about this. We have a supernatural parent who loves us and wants what's best for us. Our Spirit Father created us and does not expect us to live a spiritual life in the earthly realm using sheer human willpower—*it's impossible!* Your true *self* resides in a human body and what is natural is not spirit. If it were possible for us to transcend our human existence on our own, there would be no need for instructions from the spirit realm.

I describe the BIBLE as **B**asic **I**nstruction **B**efore **L**eaving **E**arth. Although there are many books written by different people over centuries in time, the messages are consistent. The stories are historical. Evidence exists that they really happened. What the Bible reveals is that "self" is at the inner core of our human nature, growing us from the inside out into the fullness of our spiritual being. Mankind was created to display good character traits.

Our Spirit Father wants to know that He can trust mankind to wisely use the gifts he has given us. This trust requires us to live in harmony with seven basic spiritual principles. What are these seven principles? The New Testament calls them the fruit of the Spirit.

When a person lives a life focused on the spirit realm, the seeds of good character that were planted in us before birth begin to sprout.

Attitude and behavior are the results of the soul and spirit working in perfect alignment deep within us. We can't do this on our own.

In 1995, a man named Daniel Goldman argued how people manage their emotions and relationships is important to personal and business success. He called this skill Emotional Intelligence.

The only thing in the world we can control is ourselves. The "way" we react to a situation will always determine how other people respond to us. Reaction is what matters.

Every interaction is about "how" we communicate; "what" we communicate, and "who" we communicate with. If the message we share is understood and valued, then the response from others will depend on how the message is received.

How Well Do You Communicate?

Understood – . Communication is an exchange of ideas. If someone doesn't understand what you have to say, then you've wasted your time. Carefully evaluate the situation before you speak. Look at the situation from the other person's point of view. Think about the different options before you make a choice and before you act.

Valued – Make certain the person you are talking to recognizes the importance and relevance of what you have to say. What may be important to you may not be important to the other person. Keep in mind that everyone has different values. Respect other opinions.

Act Upon –Emotionally intelligent people know how to manage their feelings. They don't automatically assume that every situation is a problem. To avoid being acted upon, they act first with intelligent information that influences decision-making. Emotionally intelligent people have compassion and empathy when reacting.

Scripture tells us that intelligence is a spiritual attribute. Our Spirit Father made previsions during our creation for mankind to have the ability to think, understand, solve problems, and make decisions. Keep in mind what I said previously: No one can make wise decisions without knowledge, understanding, and discernment.

Individuals with emotional intelligence strive to understand the emotions of others before they react. That doesn't mean they have mind control over how other people feel and behavior. It simply means they have self-control and strive to understand what makes other people tick.

A bad attitude often ties in with low self-esteem. If you can identify and understand the emotions behind bad behavior, you have a better chance of being in control of different situations. Our Spirit Father wants us to apply wisdom to the knowledge we learn. This is how ordinary people make intelligent choices. Believe me, you'll save yourself a lot of trouble if you get this right.

In the next step, our journey will take us to deeper levels of the spirit realm. In fact, you'll be introduced to our Spirit Father in the person of a human being. When He couldn't get the attention of mankind with the Old Testament, our Spirit Father created himself as an embryo and came into the physical world as a man – totally human and totally spirit. You're going to have to step outside of your comfort zone with this one, so keep an open mind.

As a child I questioned the virgin birth of Jesus. It simply didn't make sense in worldly terms, which was all I knew at the time. Even as an adult I had doubts. Now, don't get me wrong. I believed in a Spirit Father. It's the reality of a virgin birth and the resurrection of a dead man that I couldn't understand. Some things simply didn't make sense from a worldly perspective. And they never will from an earthly point of view.

Thankfully, I was awakened to the reality of a spirit realm where anything and everything is possible. Faith takes things we hope for and gives them substance or assurance. It is impossible to have faith in the promises of our Spirit Father if we look at life from a worldly perspective. I had to open the eyes of my heart to see tangible evidence of a spirit realm working for good in my everyday life.

Nothing is impossible for our Spirit Father to accomplish. Believing this Truth is a choice.

Step Five – Character
Who You Are Determines What You Do

Your journey is about to take a quantum giant leap. Taking small steps to become a whole person is no easy task, but it's a very rewarding experience. In this step we are going to talk about why perfection is impossible for human beings to achieve. There's no Scripture to support that anything in the earthly realm is perfect.

It's time to prepare your mind and body to unite with your spirit. To stay focused, take deep breaths to help your body relax while your spirit awakens. It's been dormant in your inner being for a long time. Spend another *five minutes* thinking about the good things you've done, which is the opposite of evil.

Remember the exercise you completed at the end of Step One? Go back and look at the Reality Check. This exercise provides a mirror image of YOU. Compare your Human Nature with your Spirit Nature. What you checked is who you are as an individual.

Now, go back and look at the exercise at the end of Step Two. Look at how you relate to other people. You have likes and dislikes. You make choices based on your likes and dislikes. This is who you are.

Finally, go back to Step Three and look at what people say about you. Look at the negative behavior you said is holding you back. This is also who you are.

All these qualities are distinctive to you as an individual. These character traits are how you think and behave. They say a lot about your personality. We all have positive and negative character traits because no human can ever be perfect. *Self* is attitude, behavior, strengths, weaknesses, talent, special gifts, self-concepts, emotions, and patterns of thought. *Self* is everything about you packaged in a human body. Originally, you were designed as a perfect spiritual being, but your humanness is a barrier to be your true *self.* There's an even better way to gain knowledge and understanding of *self.*

Let me take a moment to explain the difference between character and personality. Character is shaped by our beliefs and views of the world. Everyone doesn't experience life from the same perspective. Values that shape behavior and attitude can evolve to reflect what we believe. This is why a person's character and personality can change for the better or for the worse based on beliefs.

Personality describes attitude and behavior. You've probably heard the terms extrovert and introvert. These are personality traits defined by psychologists. People with extravert or introvert traits are complete opposites. The extrovert is outgoing and likes to interact with the world outside of *self*. The introvert is a quiet person who prefers to be alone in his or her inner world.

There are certain tools and techniques that psychologists and psychiatrists use to identify people as certain personality profiles. But the reality is every individual is different. *Self* is a combination of our character (what we believe and value), as well as our personality traits (behavior and attitude). While our personality is often hereditary and stored in our subconscious mind, things we value and believe have the power to reshape our character.

Let's dive a little deeper. There's a distinction between our true *self* and our personality. Keep in mind the soul is alive. Mind, emotion and free will are the soul's three functions of expression. Our human body is made of energy and this energy works in partnership with the soul to be active in the body. What we call personality is formed and stored in the subconscious mind. Think of personality as the channel the soul uses to express itself.

Personality develops from our experiences starting as babies and is influenced by our parents, customs, culture, environment, people, and circumstances. For example, people who live in low-income areas tend to carry excess baggage that influences their personality. It's difficult to see and accept life as good on Western culture when you're poor, hungry, and have low self-esteem. As human beings, we are made and unmade by our learned knowledge and thoughts. Understanding your soul begins with awareness of your personality.

My point is simple. In order to align the body with the soul and spirit, human beings need to probe the inner depths of our spiritual *self* and make change from the inside out. The focus needs to be on achieving oneness rather than trying to perfect who we are not. Part of the problem is we only see the reflection in the mirror.

The character of our Spirit Father is perfect. A starting point for character building is accepting the reality of who *self* really is. Inner living is the highest experience in creation. Our Spirit Father wants mankind to live based on hearing His voice and obeying His will. Our inner spirit has divine qualities and a will that wants to do good. This means our life has a higher purpose than what physical eyes can see.

Our Spirit Father intended for mankind to have His character but gave us the gift of choice. Unfortunately, the human personality can become disassociated with the soul and the spirit. When this happens the will of the soul to do good is blocked and the personality develops negative traits which are expressed in human behavior and attitude. The personality part of the soul is what the world sees.

Change is not something that happens automatically. Building a good character starts with the belief that mankind is connected to something greater than a physical body that gives value to *self*. Human beings must invest in their own spiritual growth by making a conscious decision to change negative personality traits. Bad habits are re-lived repeatedly in the subconscious mind. Once the conscious mind becomes aware of its deeper inner being, *self* wants to improve its character by fixing problems with its personality.

The connection needed for the soul to strengthen and for our Spirit Father's character to rule in the personality is the role of the spirit. The seeds of goodness and love are already planted in the core of *self*. And like the seed that contains the oak tree, mankind is created with the full potential of goodness, mercy, and compassion. But a supernatural power is needed to fix conditions that block the effectiveness of the spirit to do its job in the soul. In other words, when the conscious mind becomes aware that the personality needs to change, there's an awakening of the spirit that has been lying dormant within.

The human personality, embedded in the subconscious mind, is resistant to change. And so, there's a tug of war in the soul between the conscious mind and the subconscious personality that influences thoughts and feelings. Evidence of this happening is the individual becomes fearful, anxious, and wants to hold on to old habits. There's a desire to change, but the personality simply can't let go.

Self can't overcome the subconscious mind on its own. The spirit becomes the helper by connecting *the soul* with our Spirit Father, who created us in his own image and likeness in the spirit realm. This is very important to our knowing and understanding of the creation and life purpose of a man called Jesus.

We've all heard the story of the immaculate conception. As a child being prepared for the ritual of Confirmation, I had a difficult time understanding how my Spirit Father could take on the body of a man. There was only one way for an embryo to be created in a woman's womb; or so I thought at the time. The more questions I asked, the more confused I became. It was a question that haunted me well into my adulthood. Ironically, the answer was right in front of me all along. I simply had to open the eyes of my heart.

Why would I doubt the ability of a Spirit Father who is the Alpha and the Omega, who is the creator of all things visible and invisible? It's not just a matter of believing in the immaculate conception, but also understanding, accepting, and having faith in the power and authority of a supernatural Father. He not only rules everything in the spirit dimension, but the physical dimension as well. And like any parent, he wants to take on our struggles and pain.

The world outside of the spirit realm is cruel and dangerous. We humans see and live in an earthly space that is contrary to our Spirit Father's character. A world that is filled with evil thoughts and actions that affect human behavior and actions. Evil is the opposite of good and it is not eternal. It dies when the soul and spirit leave the human body. On the other hand, the goodness is perfect through all eternity. The characteristics of our Spirit Father cannot die. He is a change agent who wants to grow his human creation into the fullness of all of His glory.

Deliverance is a gift from the spirit realm. It's not something of our own doing. No human being has the power to bring the flower from the bud or the tree from the seed. All we can do is make the earthly conditions right for spiritual growth. We can't do the growing. But our Spirit Father also gave us a choice so we could or could not be obedient to His will. With awareness of the existence of a spirit realm in your conscious mind, imagine the most joyful, loving, peaceful, satisfying, and perfect relationship any human being could possibly have with a parent.

All we can do is put ourselves in a position to be blessed by our Spirit Father. As we travel along this journey searching for meaning in life, He can transform our personality and character into His own image and likeness. How is this possible? I wish I could tell you. Scientists, philosophers, and mystics have been trying to explain the workings of the spirit realm for thousands of years.

I think I've made my position very clear on the difference between a human being and a spirit being. Remember when we talked about no two things that are opposites can exist in the same space. To be totally something leaves no room for anything else.

There is only one Spirit Father who is an invisible, omnipotent, immortal, supernatural spirit who can do anything and has all-power over everything. He is not subject to physical limitations like human beings. His presence is everywhere, in both the spirit realm and the physical realm, at the same time. Everything is something and cannot be the opposite of itself, which means a soul that is totally filled with the spirit of unconditional love does not have the capacity to hate. And a spirit that is immoral is impossible to die.

The reality is that our Spirit Father wants us to understand *true self.* So, he created a spirit man with a dual nature who was unlike any other human being on earth. Jesus was totally flesh and totally spirit, existing in the same space simultaneously. He literally had a Spirit Father. Nothing else created can be totally mortal and immortal.

The man called Jesus was different. He lived on earth in the spirit realm through his conscious mind and his subconscious mind which were both perfect because he was totally spirit. His whole purpose for being was to transcend his human existence to do the will of his Spirit Father, rather than satisfy any human desires. Jesus was one of a kind.

Mankind is limited, but Jesus was not. The relationship he had with his Spirit Father is written in the New Testament. It's obvious that mankind needed a redeemer. In fact, his birth was predicted in the Old Testament. Everything you may doubt has been Truth for thousands of years. I will say it again, Jesus was one of a kind. There is no denying he was a divine spirit and soul that became flesh. His character and personality were in the image and likeness of our Spirit Father, who actually came into the physical realm in the body of a human being. There's Scripture to support this, whether you believe it or not.

Jesus knew he was going to die and even predicted his crucifixion and resurrection. The night before his suffering, Jesus gathered his disciples together to celebrate the Feast of the Passover. He followed the instructions of his Spirit Father and told them what to do in remembrance of him. Jesus had to die and be resurrected in order for his message of forgiveness and hope for eternal life to have meaning.

According to scripture, Jesus said to Martha in John 11:25-26: *"I am the resurrection and the life: he that believeth in me, though he were dead, yet shall he live, and who soever liveth and believeth in me shall never die. Believeth thou this?"*

The crucifixion must have been an intensely powerful human experience as Jesus prepared himself to unite with his Spirit Father after death. When the soldiers crucified Jesus, his body bled and died like any ordinary human being. This is vital to understand. Jesus suffered for six hours on the cross before he died because he was totally human. His death was certified by the Roman soldier who pierced him in the side with a spear and watched blood and water flow from his body.

However, unlike an ordinary human death, the soul did not leave the body of Jesus. Scripture tells us that his spirit returned to the spirit realm to unite with his Spirit Father. But, in three days the spirit of Jesus returned to the physical realm to be clothed in his resurrected body. Keep in mind Jesus was totally spirit, meaning it was impossible for him to have an eternal human death. This is why the body of Jesus was never found. I can't explain it in human terms; but I believe it.

The message of Acts 2:24 is this: **"Whom** *God hath raised up, having loosened the pains of death, because it was impossible that he should be holden of it."*

As totally human, Jesus could do nothing by himself. But by the authority of his Spirit Father, Jesus, who was totally spirit, could perform miracles. There are countless examples of this. He had already raised four people from the dead. Of course, they were totally human, meaning their bodies would eventually die again. The resurrection of Jesus was different because he was both mortal and immortal. Eternal life is the opposite of eternal death and no human, but Jesus, could be alive and dead at the same time. And so, by the authority of his Spirit Father, Jesus was able to raise his body up from death. Remember, nothing is impossible for our Spirit Father to do.

Scripture tells us that after the resurrection, Jesus still had unfinished work. There is sufficient evidence that his resurrection is Truth. Before leaving earth, Jesus spent 40 days walking and talking where his ministry had been. He was seen by multiple witnesses. This was a miracle in itself.

During his time on earth, Jesus provided mankind with specific instructions on how to obtain eternal life. The resurrected Jesus appeared first to Mary Magdelene when she discovered an empty tomb, then to two followers outside Jerusalem, and then to the eleven remaining Apostles on ten separate occasions. He appeared alive to a crowd of over 500 people. Before leaving the physical world to return to the spirit realm, Jesus gave instructions to his eleven disciples to preach the gospel to all nations. He emphasized that the gift our Spirit Father's promise to all of mankind is eternal life. We don't deserve it; nor can we earn it. Romans 6:23 says this gift is through Christ Jesus, our Lord. The gospel in the New Testament is undoubtedly *good news*.

Jesus knew the purpose of his life, death, and resurrection as Christ, the anointed one. As totally spirit sent into a physical world, Jesus clearly demonstrated how mankind can reconcile with our Spirit Father by being obedient to His will and not our own fleshly will. All He wants of human beings is for us to be just, to love kindness, and to walk humbly with Him. Why is that so hard?

Jesus let it be known that he was returning to the spirit realm so his Spirit Father could send him back into the physical realm as totally spirit to be a helper and comforter for human beings.

Jesus said in John 16:7: *Nevertheless I tell you the truth; It is expedient for you that I go away: for if I go not away, the Comforter will not come unto you; but if I depart, I will send him unto you."*

Everything that was planned for Jesus by our Spirit Father went according to His will. Let me clarify this before we go any further. Our Spirit Father is the creator of everything seen and unseen. Jesus became the human sacrifice to show humanity that the inner life is greater than the physical life. He died an earthly death as a human so we could understand our eternal destination as spirit. Jesus was totally spirit having a totally human experience.

Jesus gives basic instructions in the New Testament for mankind to have a "righteous" relationship with our Spirit Father and a "right" relationship with our fellow human beings.

Our character is shaped by what we believe is right and the actions that result from that belief. A person's attitude and behavior let us know what they stand for as an individual. Personal values not only affect the individual's life, but also impact the lives of people around that individual. Our values are stored in the subconscious mind and therefore give us a basis from which we can make decisions.

When we understand the life, death, and resurrection of Jesus, then we can live in Truth rather than an illusion of truth. I'm not talking about an emotional outburst that has people dancing in the church and screaming at our Spirit Father. Jesus Christ teachers us how to have this communication through him as an intercessor.

People who believe in Jesus Christ and follow his teachings receive his Holy Spirit to become changemakers on earth. The Bible refers to this gift as the "fruit of the Spirit."

Christian believers are distinguished from unbelievers by this fruit that produces a godly character. There are nine essential virtues of this spiritual fruit that grow in people who follow Jesus. These virtues demonstrate the character of a life submitted to the will of our Spirit Father. You'll find them in the New Testament in Galatians 5:22-23.

When the Apostle Paul talks about the "fruit of the Spirit" in Galatians he's talking about character that is produced in the believers of the life, death, and resurrection of Jesus. The word "fruit" is given to believers in its wholeness, not as individual traits. Note that verse refers to one fruit. All nine virtues provide evidence the believer is walking with Jesus and has committed *self* to allow the Holy Spirit to influence the soul. We have a choice to walk in the spirit or not to.

Scripture says there are no ungifted believers in Jesus. We can, therefore, conclude that only people living principles outlined in the New Testament of the Bible can receive the "fruit of the Spirit."

The subconscious mind can be educated to produce an outward correctness of behavior, but neither part of the mind can change the heart. Change can only be achieved through the power of the "Holy Spirit" that is like a tree rooted in the heart.

As we surrender our own will to our Spirit Father through faith in Jesus Christ, our soul becomes stronger, and our desire to do right increases. That's the difference between believers in Jesus Christ and unbelievers. Those who are believers are gifted with the Holy Spirit that bears a special fruit. We make decisions that free us from internal conflict and trouble produced by living an ungodly life. Let's look deeper at the new identity in Christ the "fruit of the spirit" produces.

1. Love

True love comes from the deepest part of our being, the heart. Everyone has the capacity to experience true love as their inheritance from our Spirit Father. The opposite of love is hate. It's love that allows us to look beyond someone's faults and see their needs. The ultimate display of true love is sacrifice. How many people do you know who would sacrifice their life for you? A parent, maybe. When we love someone without conditions, we validate their worth. The love we give and receive our Spirit Father is an unconditional reality. This selfless love is the foundation of our *becoming* like the loving character of Jesus, and everything builds on that foundation. Believers who live in the spirit of Christ love unconditionally and do things unconditionally. Love guides us to be true to *self*.

2. Joy

Joy is a spiritual characteristic designed by our Spirit Father to be much greater than happiness, especially when it is the result of experiencing something good. Unlike happiness, Joy does not depend on conditions of outside circumstances. While happiness and pleasure generate emotions that wear off, joy is a deeply-rooted, spiritual asset in the soul that is permanent. Because it is spirit, Joy can occupy the conscious and the subconscious space in the mind at the same time. Once the seed of joy is planted in the heart, nothing and no one on earth can take it away. True joy requires a total surrender of the human will. The believer has confidence that whatever happens is the will of our Spirit Father who is in total control. When we trust Him totally and completely, we have joy.

3. Peace

Resting in peace means a believer must die to the temptations of the physical world. It's human nature to be conscious of the turmoil, greed, and chaos happening around us. Especially with so much violence everywhere. Jesus said we will have trouble in the world, but not to worry. For unbelievers, thinking about this will have no effect. They don't know how to live peacefully with other people and their ungodly thoughts will always produce anxiety and trouble.

Believers, on the other hand, have the virtue of peace. Our Spirit Father produces a "rest" deep within the soul that is beyond anything the mind can ever imagine. We have peace in the time of storms.

4. Patience

It's our human nature to want to be in control of situations. But everything has its appointed time. Trouble always follows when people try to fix problems themselves without spiritual guidance. Impatient people want what they want, and they want it NOW!

Believers are just as guilty of this as nonbelievers. It's our human nature to want to be in control. Patience is a virtue that serves everyone well. It gives believers the capacity to wait for the right opportunity or the right answer that may not come right away. Our Spirit Father wants us to slow us down, to wait patiently without frustration, and to trust Him. Patience comes in handy for believers who have a habit of making quick decisions.

5. Kindness

Kindness is something we learn as children. Can you remember being taught this? "Do unto others as you want them to do unto you." Unfortunately, this lesson is lost as we grow up in a cold, hateful world. People have forgotten how to be kind to one another. Kindness isn't just a personality trait. In the believer, it flows from the heart and generates trust from others.

No one can say they are a follower of Jesus Christ and have a mean spirit. Kindness and hardheartedness can't occupy the same space. For the believer kindness is the foundation for many relationships, including family, friends, marriage, business acquaintances, and more. It's the nice things we do that count. Maybe that's why acts of kindness are mentioned so often in Scripture.

6. Goodness

The goodness described in the Holy Bible as fruit of the Spirit is something worth sharing with others. It demonstrates both kindness and faithfulness. Before you can really understand this gift, you must know what it means to have a pure heart.

When a believer is striving for a higher spiritual life, the heart is considered the center of both love and wisdom. The believer is still human, and humans are not perfect beings. We make mistakes.

Just because believers think from the heart and love from the mind, doesn't mean we don't make mistakes. We fall and get back up again. Goodness must be practiced every day. The believer's goodness gives life to *doing* things that go beyond the people we love.

7. Faithfulness

Scripture says faith is having confidence in what we hope for and assurance in what we cannot see. The opposite of faith is disbelief. We live in a culture that demands evidence in order to have rational belief. It's our human nature to have doubt. If we can't see it and can't prove it's true, then the mind will struggle with doubt. Yet, there is evidence all around us of a supernatural, Spirit Father who is faithful to us, loves us unconditionally, and looks for faithfulness and unconditional love in return. Without faith there is doubt, which typically results in disobedience.

Faith is at the heart of spiritual development. In Hebrews 11:1, the Bible says that *FAITH* is being sure of what we hope for and having complete trust in what we don't see. To truly embrace our destiny of eternal life when the body dies, we must have Faith in the spirit realm and live according to how the "Living Word" tells us to live.

8. Gentleness

Meekness does not mean weakness. It refers to an attitude. Jesus said the meek will inherit the earth. He is the greatest role model of a meek character that ever lived on earth. Gentleness is how someone acts when they are meek; they are slow to anger. It takes a strong soul for a human being to be meek enough to care for people and not expect anything in return. Arrogance is the opposite of Gentleness.

Humility is necessary for self-improvement. A person has to be meek before a change toward goodness can happen. Only by being humble can we realize we don't know everything, and we don't need everything. Once a believer discovers it's possible to exist in the world, but not become worldly minded, that person is ready to be transformed by the Holy Spirit. Scripture says the character of Jesus was a man who was gentle and humble at heart. He lived not for himself, but for others.

9. Self-Control

Why do some people know how to divert their attention away from temptation, while others only live for the moment? It's because human nature craves instant gratification. The opposite of self-control is self-indulgence or unruliness. Some people want what they want and will do anything to get it. In a way this is like taking drugs. When a person can't have what they want, they look for a pacifier.

Only through the work of the Holy Spirit can a believer control what happens naturally. Anger, for example, is an emotion that causes people to lose self-control and act without thinking. For the believer, it's not about how to handle anger that makes the difference. It's the ability to control thoughts, emotions, and actions that reflect what Jesus would do. It's the believer who can bring self-discipline and wise decisions to the surface in a difficult situation, not the ungodly. Self-control is a gift of the spirit.

Our Spirit Father wants to guide mankind to a path that leads to more fullness in life. Humans have become confused by what that really means. It's not about a path that leads to fortune, power, and fame. Rich people are just as unhappy as poor people. They can buy all the material things they want, but they can't buy their way into the spirit realm. The point is money can buy comfort and stuff, but it can't buy what is spiritual. True abundant life has an overflow of unconditional love, unspeakable joy, everlasting peace, and all the rest of the fruit of the Spirit. Best of all is the promise of eternal life in the spirit realm.

Jesus commands his followers to love our Spirit Father and to love our neighbor. This translates into loving our enemies, returning good for evil, and blessing those who mistreat us. Yes, this is a difficult pill to swallow for an ordinary human being. It's not our human nature to love the unlovable. The good news is that every believer has access to the fruit of the Spirit to grow inwardly and become spiritually mature. When our human nature fails, the indwelling Holy Spirit will always save us. Being in touch with the heart creates hope.

The fruit of the Spirit is a gift to develop a strong character. This gift not only helps the believer to do the right thing, but also to care about others. Making a mistake doesn't mean a person doesn't have good character. Everyone makes mistakes. But there's a path that any human being can take that offers hope and a more meaningful future.

Let's review what you've learned on this journey so far.

1. We are spirit beings having a _____ experience.

2. Emotions, Mind and Will are elements of the _____.

3. Our true self is mind, body, and _____.

4. Character is shaped by our _____ and view of the world.

5. Habits are stored in the _____ mind.

6. People who lack a sense of _____ have significantly worse mental health and physical health.

7. A person with low _____ never sees or accepts what is considered good.

8. Personality describes attitude and _____.

9. The character of our Spirit _____ is perfect.

10. Conditional _____ is an emotion based on need.

Answers: 1. human. 2. soul. 3. spirit. 4. beliefs. 5. subconscious; 6. purpose.
7. self-esteem. 8. behavior. 9. Father. 10. love.

Step Six – Purpose
Know The Reason Why You Exist

By now it should be clear that life is a journey of growing and becoming; of letting go of past habits to experience a renewing of your mind. As we look at the path ahead, it's obvious we're going into a whole new dimension. In this step we'll discuss what it means to have purpose and to live intentionally.

It's time to prepare your mind and body to take another giant leap on your path to empowerment and personal change. To stay focused, take deep breaths to help your body and soul relax while your spirit awakens to a sense of purpose. Spend another *five minutes* thinking about the good things you've done. Once you are relaxed and ready to focus, start seeing *self* through a spiritual lens.

One of the most frustrating experiences in life is failing to know why we exist. Earlier this year I attended a conference at the Faith Center in Florida called "Maximizing Your Potential." A woman sat down next to me and said, "I have no idea why I was born!" The world is filled with people like that. I never saw her again. So, by the time the conference was over I had a revelation to write this book.

Everyone has a need to feel valued, and to know that their living is not in vain. In short, we all want to know why we were created and what we are expected to do with our life.

As you question your own existence, what talents and abilities come to mind? Your personality reveals a lot about gifts that were given to you by our Spiritual Father during your creation. You were destined to do something just to prove His glory. Talents are what people can do naturally, like leading others or being smart with numbers. It's what you've always been able to do well. Abilities are skills you had to develop over time, like reading and writing. It's what you have learned and have worked hard to develop with good execution. Singing is a talent while self-control is a skill.

Most people have all the talent and skills they need to get by in life. Of course, there are some activities where people have the ability to perform better than their peers. Look back at your past and think of things you were always good at doing. The people who know you best probably recognize your hidden talents.

Unfortunately, what happens is the subconscious mind becomes fixed on accumulating worldly stuff. Human nature is focused on using talent and skills to build the ego, rather than divine reasoning to help others. This creates a cloud of disappointment and doubt, which results in a lack of purpose in life. One disappointment leads to another, until confusion takes over and people don't bother to think about what they are doing or why they are doing it. And when their expectations aren't met, they feel...trapped.

At some point along this journey called life we all question the purpose of our existence. Why were we born? This usually happens when we've become so preoccupied with the world that we've lost sight of who true *self* really is. The mind, body and spirit are out of alignment. Far too often we live by our sensory experiences without thinking about the consequences. We are willing to pay any price to do what we want and get what we want when we want it.

For example, people who have premarital sex may well face the consequence of having a child out of wedlock. Lust gets pregnant and has a baby. People who drink and drive may well experience the consequence of a DUI. Fun gets thirsty and consumes too much alcohol while having a good time. There's an outcome for every action, but we may not see the link when making choices.

People who don't think before they act tend to blame others when things go wrong—the cop who issued the DUI; the boyfriend who got the girl pregnant; or "God" who lets bad things happen to good people. They condition their soul (emotions, mind, and will) to live with chronic stress and anxiety. And they constantly need pacifiers to ease the pain. Our Spirit Father doesn't put temptation in the way to test us. Temptation is self-created. It comes from the subconscious mind in each of us and only from us.

We have freedom to make our own choices and cannot blame anyone else for the outcome. Bad things happen because we're human. The important thing is to know how to avoid trouble, as well as how to endure devastation that can be an outcome.

The fact that you've come this far on your journey is an accomplishment. Keep in mind that you're at the very beginning of your transformation. Spiritual growth takes time and self-mastery. In fact, there's no earthly destination. You may have meaningful goals that drive your everyday life, but these are only part of your journey. Your life isn't over when goals are met. And depending on how you live, your journey isn't over when your body dies.

Your spiritual journey is all about what you experience along the way – the good, the bad, and the ugly. Whether you recognize it or not, your living has a positive or negative impact in the world. Every thought, word, and action are experiences that are both internal and external. And this is why every life matters.

Your purpose on earth has a lot to do with how you deal with other people. In fact, without other people you wouldn't need a purpose. Our Spirit Father created you as a human to make an extraordinary impact doing something good for His glory.

When I first decided to write this book, I had a vision. I wanted to awaken 100,000 young people to their hidden potential so they can have a life-changing human experience. I was concerned that far too many teens and young adults have destructive behavior that can only lead to a negative future.

I told my pastor about my concern. I said, "Bishop, millions of youth today are lost and I don't know what to do. I'm too old to make a difference." His response was an awakening for me.

He said, "You're never too old to have a purpose. Find other people your age who aren't satisfied with what is happening to our young people and do something." At the age of 77, my Spirit Father sent me a message on how to be a difference maker. So, I wrote two books: *The People Zoo* and *The Deliverance Project*.

I see my books as an intervention. Over the next year, with the guidance of the Holy Spirit, I plan to empower 100,000 youth to be agents of change in their communities. How youth deal with situations and circumstances really matters. They can live for years with stress, anxiety, and pacifiers; or they can have a vision that moves them to a greater purpose as a follower of Jesus.

Youth with a sense of purpose in life tend to perform better in school and experience higher self-esteem. The problem is that the ego is always a barrier to doing our Spirit Father's will. In a crazy, mixed-up world, young people desire to be in control, but don't understand there are limitations to free will. Humans can't simply do what they want without consequences.

If you're wondering how to find your purpose, whether you're young, old or somewhere in between, start with a vision. Think about a good cause that needs benevolent love. A vision will give life to your motivation. It's a glimpse of what you want to produce or accomplish with the end in mind. This is an important point: no individual can fulfill their purpose without digging down deep to find inner strength. At the beginning you will have doubts because that's how your subconscious mind has been conditioned. Fear is normal, so don't be discouraged. Keep the faith and a spirit within you will walk alongside you as a helper and a friend. You won't see Jesus, but your heart will know he's there.

The key is to have faith. Purpose will produce the fruit of the Spirit, to live a life of love, joy, peace, patience, kindness, goodness, faithfulness, gentleness, and self-control. When you have the gift of this fruit within, you can build on its virtues in your soul (emotions, mind and will). You don't have to be a slave to your subconscious mind where habits are stored. Fear and doubt will be overcome when your conscious mind is focused on your purpose.

Scripture says: **"But *they that wait upon the Lord shall renew their strength; they shall mount up with wings as eagles; they shall run, and not be weary; and they shall walk, and not faint."***

Isaiah 40:31

This is one of my favorite verses from the Old Testament. It gives me confidence that I can accomplish any task that will fulfill my purpose, no matter how difficult.

I love the story about the prophet named Isaiah. He lived many centuries before the birth of Jesus. It was a time when the people of Judea had turned their backs on their Spirit Father who had brought them out of slavery in Egypt. The people had become wicked human beings. They were using the gift of free will to do their own thing without fear of any consequences. Like today, it was a terrible time in history. The Book of Isiah is filled with warnings about judgement and salvation.

According to Scripture, Isaiah called on all nations to see the authority of our Spirit Father as the Alpha and Omega, who in the beginning and the end is both judge and savior. He warned that Israel would face dire consequences for its rebellion. Isaiah even condemned the corrupt politicians who cared more about money and power than justice. (It's amazing how history repeats itself.)

Although Isaiah preached a message of repentance he received from the spirit realm, the people of Judeah refused to hear it. But the prophet's message wasn't all doom and gloom. Isaiah also prophesied of a coming savior; a man who would be despised, rejected, and afflicted; that he would carry our sorrows; and would be wounded for our transgressions. Isaiah predicted the coming of a Messiah who would redeem his people for their wrongdoings.

Now let's fast forward about seven hundred years. Jesus referred to himself as the "son of man," meaning he was totally human like you and I. But unlike us, he was totally spirit, meaning he had the authority, through our Spirit Father to be in total control of his body and his environment. He could unearth the spirit that was within him to live on earth in perfect obedience to do our Father's will.

No other human but Jesus has ever been created as a divine being, with powers that allowed him to perform miracles. His purpose for being the "son of man" was to reveal the reality of the spirit realm to humanity. Jesus was born to lead us through the struggles of everyday living so that in death, the soul and the spirit (*self*) can go back to the Spirit Father who created us. In other words, Jesus came into the physical realm to demonstrate how humans can have total control over the human body. His purpose was to offer his human body as a living sacrifice against evil, and then resurrect it into eternal life to prove that we are spirit having a human experience.

Jesus sacrificed his body, his sinless life, to become an intercessor in the spirit realm on our behalf. What a token of love! He entered the spirit realm to appear before our Spirit Father on behalf of all mankind. And with an everlasting love, Jesus Christ still has only one purpose – to set our captive souls free of worldly temptations.

Note that I used the title Christ in my description of Jesus. The word Christ comes from the Greek word "Christo," meaning the anointed one. This is critical to understand. Jesus was the son of man. He was human with a body. Christ was his divine nature.

As a Jew, Jesus was raised according to laws in the Old Testament. There was no such religion as Christianity during his time on earth. Jesus came to save the Jews and they despised and rejected him.

Knowing the weaknesses of human beings, our Spirit Father sent the divine spirit of Jesus back into the physical realm to give our soul (mind, emotion, and free will) strength to overcome worldly flesh. He doesn't force humans to obey His will. Because he loves us unconditionally, we have freedom to follow Jesus or reject him.

To make everything simple for the human mind to understand, Christians believe Jesus is the Messiah who was prophesied in the Old Testament, giving him the title of Christ (the anointed one).

Christians believe you can only have eternal life in the spirit realm though faith in Jesus Christ. Jews believe they enter the spirit realm though their good works. Jews follow the Torah, the first five books of the Bible which are attributed to Moses. They follow the teachings of Moses to this day. Christians believe in the gospel of the New Testament and follow the teachings of Jesus Christ.

The four gospels in the New Testament were written by Matthew, Mark, Luke, and John who were disciples of Jesus. All four gospels tell the same story – that Jesus is the Jewish Messiah who was promised in the Old Testament. You don't have to be a Christian to read the Bible. And you have the free will to choose what to believe.

However, not believing in anything is how people get lost in this journey called life. They have no idea where they are going, where they are supposed to be, or what they are supposed to do. I'd rather have divine direction and purpose for my life.

Scripture tells us that nothing exists for itself; everything in creation has a purpose—including humans. Just because we don't recognize the guidance of Jesus Christ doesn't mean he isn't real. Accept him as your savior and he will be with you. The Holy Spirit directs our human life to do the will of our Spirit Father.

Even the prisoner on death row, who serves as an example of the consequences of ill-chosen decisions, is being used for a purpose. We all make mistakes and sometimes our biggest regret is that we can't undo the past. But selflessness is inherent in parental love. Our Spirit Father is forgiving. No one person in all the earth is outside of His love and goodness. That's why He provides for His children.

As a Divine Being, our Spirit Father has power over every aspect of our lives and indwells each individual with a fragment of his divinity. I'm not saying that humans are designed to be robots who automatically exhibit the perfect moral character of our Spirit Father. I'm just trying to awaken you to the fact that we are all spirit having a human experience. This is why Jesus was called the "son of man." His human nature had a deep guiding purpose as well as a destiny for his earthly existence. Jesus knew instinctively what is right and had the authority to dominate over his own body and environment.

Unlike other humans, Jesus didn't have a choice to do wrong. As a divine being, his will and our Spirit Father's will were one and the same. There were no opposite choices in his soul (mind, emotions, and free will) because he was totally spirit in a human body.

You don't have to be religious to believe that Jesus lived from the inward out, as a human being. Although he was the son of man (human), the divine spirit of our Spirit Father was *indwelled in* Jesus giving him power to become a change agent in the world. Even people who have never read the Bible can recognize an inner voice that tells us right from wrong. Our Spirit Father gives us freedom to choose the path of life we want to follow. Jesus didn't have a choice.

Seeking to understand the life and death of Jesus is probably the most important decision anyone can make. I know it was for me. When I made my Confirmation at the age of ten, I was motivated to be good. I saw that flash of light when the Bishop put his hands on my head, and immediately had a revelation. I was a valued believer in Jesus Christ. But I wasn't quite there yet in terms of spiritual growth. Let's face it, I was still a kid with a lot of maturing to do. Furthermore, nobody told me that bad things can happen to good people. Without awareness of *self*, my adult life was very crazy.

I suppose my journey is no different than other people who are challenged with difficult situations. We want total control over our lives and don't always make the right decisions. It's difficult to trust someone you can't see. Still, my Spirit Father has been ever faithful.

The same year that I made my Confirmation, I caught walking pneumonia and almost died. But my faith in Jesus kept me.

I married an atheist at the age of eighteen and was divorced by the time I was twenty-two. But my faith in Jesus kept me.

I got married again to a Christian minister and eighteen years later he left me for another woman. But my faith in Jesus kept me.

I had a child from each marriage and never received a penny of child support from ex-husbands. But my faith in Jesus kept me.

I married again, this time to a gambler and lost my home, my business, and my savings. But my faith in Jesus kept me.

I waited ten years before I married again, this time to my current husband of twenty-three years. And my faith in Jesus blessed me.

Scripture gives us a glimpse of who we *really* are and the spiritual dimension that is open to us; but it takes the Holy Spirit to tell each of us what we are supposed to do and why. Now common sense would tell anybody not to marry an atheist, a playboy preacher, or a gambler. Believe me when I say Christians don't always use common sense. Human nature tells us not to listen to the inner voice that says, "Don't do it!" I loved being married, but I didn't have the patience to wait on the Lord to send me the right husband. I was lonely and my emotions took me down the wrong path more than once.

There are lots of verses in both the Old Testament and the New Testament that describe a spiritual path that leads to purpose. Once we clearly understand what our Spirit Father expects of our life, it's possible the world around us will never be the same. History is filled with examples of ordinary people who found their "God-given" purpose and changed society for the better.

One of mankind's greatest gifts from our Spirit Father is the power of choice. I know of nothing else in the universe that was created with this gift except human beings. Everywhere we look in the universe we see evidence of an orderly presence of a divine intelligence. This awesome power brings the trees from the seed, the flower from the bud, and the corn from the blade.

Truthfully speaking, nothing in creation grows of its own accord—including humans. The message that Jesus brought from the spirit realm is that we are not sufficient unto ourselves. We have a Spirit Father who is in total control and has total power over every aspect of living and unliving things. He makes old things new, and He's always creating new things. He has a purpose for anything and everything we humans encounter during our earthly existence. Greatness belongs exclusively to our Spirit Father. No one can become great unless He destines for it to happen.

A person's continuous life on earth is no coincidence; it is not a matter of chance. It was planned and ordained by a higher order of intelligence than our human mind has the capacity to understand.

One way we can be assured of a spiritual presence in our lives is by gaining knowledge of our Spirit Father's purpose for life and death. Scriptures tell us that death is the consequence of making the wrong choices. Romans 5:12 call these bad choices "sin."

Physical death occurs in the body when the vital functions of the organs cease to operate. At this point, depending on the status of the inner life, the soul and the spirit are separated from the human body. The believer's spirit and soul experience life after death because they are raised by the eternal spirit of Jesus Christ. Scripture assures Christians that their earthly body will be shed to receive a new immortal body. The believer will be with Jesus Christ forever.

On the other hand, the effect of "sin" on the unbeliever is that life ends as an entire entity—body, soul, and spirit. Remember when we talked about opposites can't exist in the same space at the same time. Evil separates man from his Creator and the possibility of eternal life. Therefore, when the human body dies, its spiritual existence also experiences death. In other words, the soul dies too.

As you read, it's important to recognize the difference between termination and transition, and between life and death. Life implies survival whereas death implies an ending.

Our Spirit Father cares about the outcome of every human life. He wants us to rely on His provision and trust in His guidance. He wants His grace to be sufficient for us. He is our Father in the highest possible terms that can be expressed in human language. (Notice that I use capital letters to acknowledge His authority).

The miracle of grace isn't something we should take for granted. Grace can best be described as our Spirit Father's generosity toward us, and His loving favor given to those who obey Him. Of course, this is an expression of grace in human terms, the only terms I know. Our human understanding of living by grace means trusting in the promises of Jesus Christ.

Our Spirit Father doesn't guarantee an easy life, but He does gift us the fruit of the Spirit as a guide to live by.

What is critical to remember is that His promises are always related to His purpose. We don't deserve any of our Spirit Father's blessings, and we certainly can't earn them. Our human efforts, no matter how religious or moral, can never gain the grace that comes from our Spirit Father's mercy and love. He will only support us if whatever we do is in *His* intended purpose. In other words, we must cooperate and be obedient to be pleasing in His sight.

A purposeful life has direction and guidance. When our Spirit Father has a plan, He also provides for its fulfillment. What happens is this—when we don't respect the purpose of a gift, we often misuse it. We humans are not born to automatically be in sync with our Spirit Father's specific intention. Although we are created for His purpose, He gives us freedom to choose our own path in life.

What causes us to sometimes be indecisive and take the wrong path is our fear of failure; we're afraid of what others may think. Instead of relying on our Spirit Father's provisions, we give in to our emotions, take control, and wind up making the wrong choices.

I'm telling you that our Spirit Father doesn't expect us to be perfect beings. Hear me out; this is vitally important. Many people die without ever forgiving themselves for making mistakes. Again, this is because we are human. It's also why our Spirit Father has a plan for our restoration. He uses mistakes to refine us. He uses values to test us; disappointments to humble us; failures to motivate us; frustrations to strengthen us, and disobedience to grow our faith. So, don't be discouraged because you messed up. You are not the only one. His restoration process is how our Spirit Father prepares us to become better people and to do what He intended for our life. Even in our mess He knows we have the potential to fulfill a purpose.

The desire of most parents is for their children to make wise decisions and make best use of their talents. Our Spirit Father is no different. He wants to save us from the consequences of bad choices. His salvation is a gift to us. Without His grace and mercy, no person can be saved. We humans aren't equipped with the power to save ourselves without help from the spiritual realm.

The Bible says that "all have sinned and come short of the glory of God." It also says the punishment for sin is death. Think about this. Our Father has the power to take our life at any time. We have all been repeatedly disobedient in one way or another—in thought, words, actions and avoiding to act. Each of us deserves to be punished for our wrong doings. We know it. We even accept it. However, no one wants the maximum punishment, which from our Spirit Father's perspective is spiritual disconnection when the body dies. Eternal life is off the table as an ultimate reward for obedience.

Judging this punishment by earthly standards can be very deceiving because society's laws allow for different degrees of punishment for crimes. In our Spirit Father's eyes, no wrongdoing is greater or smaller than the other. A lie is as much an evil act as a murder—evil is evil. The punishment established by our Spirit Father is death and total disconnection from His life-giving power.

The first thing we say when we find ourselves in need of help is, "Lord, have mercy!" We know who is in control and we all look to our Spirit Father to save us. We don't want to get the punishment we really deserve. His mercy is what forgives us. And no matter what we do, He still loves us. If we're truly sorry, no matter how far we've strayed from the path of a meaningful life, He will bring us back and set us on the right track. That's what parents do.

Humans need to stop taking mercy and grace for granted. We must acknowledge that we can do nothing ourselves. This is the whole point of my writing this book. We can ask for forgiveness for any wrongful behavior, but mercy can only come from our Spirit Father. We experience His grace and mercy when the punishment is not as severe as we expected, or it simply isn't doled out at all.

There is no way, apart from Jesus Christ, to be saved from the consequences of wrongdoing. The New Testament says that Jesus Christ is the only way to our Spirit Father. Trust me when I tell you this is Truth. Jesus, the son of man, was able to walk among the evil doers to teach them. However, He didn't become like the evil doers and do the things they did. He simply could not.

The sole purpose of the life of Jesus was for our Spirit Father to become human with all the attributes of a fleshly person. Through Jesus, the son of man, our Spirit Father could teach his children how to have life and have it more abundantly. Spirit took on human flesh to teach things to us in terms we can understand.

Jesus was a missionary, teaching the fundamental principles of living intentionally in spirit and in Truth. Jesus, the son of man, died an earthly death as a human. The last words he cried out from the cross were: "It is finished!" Jesus had completed his purpose. Through the death of Jesus, our Father had provided mankind with an eternal destination for our spirit self. Jesus became the human sacrifice to show us that the inner life is greater than the outer life.

This is basic instructions we read throughout the Bible—how to have a "righteous" relationship with our Creator. This is the path to an abundant life, as well as how to having a "right" relationship with our fellow humans; the way to have a peaceful co-existence on earth. Why is that so hard for humans to do?

Of course, we can't live out our Spirit Father's instructions if we don't know it. Merely living a good life, no matter how much "good" we may do, can save none of us. Not everyone believes or accepts this philosophy. Jews are still waiting for their Messiah. And I'm waiting for mine to come back into the world as he promised he would.

The Bible says we can only be saved by faith in Jesus Christ. This point can't be emphasized enough. We are saved by what we believe. My faith is in a personal savior who is the intercessor that connects me to my Spirit Father and to my God-given purpose.

Jesus Christ, through his eternal Spirit, leads mankind down a path that takes us beyond mere survival, to rise above the level of our animal nature, to exist in another dimension of life.

Faith and belief in the teachings of Jesus Christ and following in His footsteps is what brings us into a personal relationship with our Spirit Father. We express our faith by the way we live.

The Holy Spirit can then work within our lives and bring forth the fruit of the Spirit to change our lives. Again, I'm using capital letters to respect and emphasize this authority.

The Bible prepares us for a higher level of existence. And once we get into the practice of reading and applying messages from the spirit realm, the Holy Spirit will guide us to finding the *real* reason for our existence. It's called living with purpose.

If our time here on earth is not used to fulfill our God-given purpose, then our life is wasted, and our living has been in vain. As Christians, we all have a religious obligation to follow Christ, to live according to instructions from our Spirit Father. When we believe His Word, we must be submissive to His will and His way. There's nothing mysterious about this. The fundamental key to having joy is the discovery of a sense of purpose for your life and using your talent and skills to fulfill that purpose.

Our Spirit Father wants us to be reborn of the spirit; living to honor and show Him obedience. Naturally, the idea of being submissive and making changes in attitude and behavior to someone you can't meet face to face can be very intimidating. Mankind's resistance to change is so inherent in the human personality that it could almost be considered second nature. In fact, it might lead some people reading this book to doubt the very existence of a Spirit Father and also question the divinity of Jesus. When we deal with doubt, we are especially vulnerable to worldly temptation.

The very thought of surrendering all freedom requires an internal struggle. There's no greater battle any human will ever fight in the soul (mind, emotions, and free will). The key to winning spiritual warfare is to always keep this in mind: **Our Father reveals truth to us in His Word; Christ lives within us to act on His Word, and the Holy Spirit enables us to live out His Word.** He's an awesome Spirit Father who wants only the best for His children. When our lives are rooted and grounded in the teachings of Jesus Christ, we become what we think. We become Christ-like.

Sometimes it seems like the harder we try to do good the more temptations we encounter. That's because worldly forces don't want us to surrender to the spirit realm. The war between good and evil is a reality. Knowing and obeying our Spirit Father's will is an effective weapon against any temptation. As believers, we must be committed to following a life governed by the gospel of Jesus Christ and living intentionally in spirit and in Truth.

We exist in a culture today that is careless about the value of human life. Our earthly society seems to have lost its sense of purpose. So, it's not surprising that many people reading this book may not be concerned about pursuing their purpose in life. It's probably the last thing they want to think about. But avoiding truth doesn't change Truth; it simply means people have freedom to turn away if they choose.

With that said, let's look at the purpose of the church. Everything has a reason for its existence. Jesus brought people together to praise and glorify our Spirit Father in worship. He also nurtured them with the "Living Word" that has become the New Testament. That's the purpose of the church. Throughout modern history the church has been the body of Christ -- a place for believers to meet and grow together; to become Christ-like. Christianity is a family thing.

There may be different dimensions of Christianity, but the one thing that unites us as one body in Christ is the Holy Spirit. As members of one family, we cherish our relationship with our Spirit Father and our brother, Jesus Christ. We also value the unique characteristics of the Christian life.

We know that our Spirit Father loves us, provides for us, forgives us, and promises to reward our faithfulness with eternal life. There is no death for the *true* believers. The mission of the church is to prepare the way for our Spirit Father's Kingdom on earth. We become members of His Christian family by accepting Jesus Christ as our personal Savior and believing that our evil ways are forgiven through Him.

Once we confess our faith, Our Spirit Father prepares us to fulfill our purpose in life by embedding the fruit of the Spirit within us. He also gives us gifts that are meant for Christians to use in serving one another and not for our own self-edification.

Misusing these gifts for personal gratification has serious consequences. Unfortunately, too many so-called Christians play religious games, using spiritual gifts to build their own kingdom. As Christians we are expected to enhance the spiritual growth of our brothers and sisters in Christ. This expectation is always shortsighted when seen from a human perspective and not with the heart.

We have special gifts and talents only because our Spirit Father gives them to us. There is no excuse for any Christian to use these gifts in spiritual disobedience. Our relationship with our Spirit Father through Christ must be mutually beneficial.

If our time here on earth is not used to fulfill its intended purpose, our life is wasted and lost. Our Spirit Father has a plan for each individual and provides for its fulfillment. Think about the skills and talents you have received from Him. The truth is you already have what you need to turn things around. The trick is just doing it; taking that first step to make it happen.

List below your God-given talents and skills if you know them.

1. _____

2. _____

3. _____

4. _____

5. _____

Now consider how you can use these gifts for good. It's necessary to think more deeply about who you are and what you've accomplished. The past few years have been filled with life lessons. Things you wish you had done and things you wish you had done differently.

Only when we take action and apply what we've learned from life's lessons will things begin to change for the better.

Imagine looking back over your adult life. Below explain what you like about things you've accomplished:

_____

_____

_____

_____

_____

What do you wish you had done differently?

_____

_____

_____

_____

Ask our Father to reveal to you His purpose for your life.

_____

_____

_____

_____

Step Seven - Breakthrough
Making A Choice To Change

By now, you should have insight into your journey's beginning and the end of life on earth. You've been introduced to a Spirit Father who created you before you came into the world. He's the one who will bring your spirit home when your body dies. The Bible has powerful instructions on how to rise above worldly circumstances through an inseparable spiritual connection. We can't see the energy that flows to us through a mediator named Jesus, but we can feel it. In this final lesson you'll learn how to call on Jesus and he will answer. And if you haven't figured out your purpose by now, this final step will give you a clue.

Our Spirit Father's ultimate purpose is for each of us to make a positive difference in the life of another person. His desire is for human beings to use spiritual gifts, talents, and skills to do good. Your life on earth will never make sense until you fulfill this purpose.

In the movie "The Passion of Christ," we see the most realistic version of Jesus, the son of man, suffering on the cross. The film primarily covers the final 12 hours before the death of Jesus. This human experience is known as "the Passion." The whole meaning of the movie is to show us the supernatural end of all creation, which is an spiritual reunion with our Creator. The life journey of Jesus on earth was to show us inseparable connection with our Spirit Father.

The New Testament describes the incredible relationship between Jesus and the spirit realm. Our Spirit Father had a plan that included the baptism of Jesus, his anointing, his last supper, his arrest, his trail, his suffering, his crucifixion, his death, his burial, and his resurrection. From the beginning to the end, the purpose of Jesus coming into the earth was for absolute goodness to overcome evil that despised him and killed him. Jesus chose to die because he was totally spirit with an inseparable connection to the will of our Spirit Father.

Jesus had the power to escape death because he was immortal. There's a logical answer to those who question the resurrection. We know Jesus had a dual nature. He was one of a kind – both man and the spirit of our Father embedded in human flesh. Love, which is the total opposite of hate, is immortal and cannot die. Jesus was created to reunite mankind with our Spirit Father through the ultimate sacrifice of his own mortal body so he could return as the Holy Spirit.

If you haven't watched the movie "The Passion of Christ," you should. As a mortal human being, Jesus was bruised, beaten, and broken so mankind can have healing and wholeness in every area of life. His death was a breakthrough. As humans, we are not strong enough to have the fulness of joy that our Spirit Father possesses. He resurrected Jesus to return him to earth as a mediator on our behalf.

In the previous step I stated that greatness belongs exclusively to our Spirit Father. No one can become great unless He destines for it to happen. According to Scripture, our Spirit Father highly exalted Jesus Christ as Lord of His church and gave him a name which is above all names. **"That at the name of Jesus every knee shall bow, of things in heaven, and things in earth, and things under the earth; And that every tongue should confess that Jesus Christ is Lord, to the glory of God the Father."**

-   *Philippians 2:10-11*

We are living in a time when human beings have the hardest of hearts. Evil is everywhere. All over the world people want power and wealth and will do anything to get these things. In the past, humans would hide their negative qualities. Today, people are being driven by evil they seem unable to control. True believers understand what our Spirit Father is doing on earth. We know there's a purpose for good in all that He does. The Book of Revelations is being fulfilled.

Jesus came from a spirit world that is greater and more perfect than the earthly one we live in. In eternity, Jesus has an immortal life that he also promises for us. We can't see spiritual realities with the human eye, but we also know there's a place on earth for refuge and strength. A place where faith, hope, love, peace, kindness, and trust can be experienced deep within the heart. Only through the spirit that dwells deep within can a human being give up evil thoughts and actions and move the soul to a new level of goodness on earth.

Humans have an animal nature that interacts with the physical world through our five senses. We've talked about this before in previous steps. What differentiates humans from animals is our ability to think and to reason, to know the difference between good and evil and to take control of our humanity.

Like animals, humans have certain instincts that can control our behavior. I introduced some of these animal-like personalities in my book *The People Zoo – A Guide To Know Who You're Talking To*. Animal nature is the lowest level of existence for any human being. People living at this level have lost total control of their body and soul. Instead of taking action to elevate their thinking, they allow their mind to be controlled by emotions and their five senses. They are missing the reason they were created. A life on this level is wasted.

Before you can be delivered from evil, you need to understand that deliverance means different things to different people. As human beings we can never become perfect, like Jesus. He was created one of a kind, equal in spirit with his humanity. But humans can become whole. Rather than live a life that is fragmented and disjointed, we can train the conscious mind to be aligned with Christ-like principles. Of course, no one can do this on their own. Mankind's animal nature will always be dominant in the physical realm to elicit fear and doubt; to act aggressive and greedy. But human beings were created to have dominion over the animals, not to act like them. And the choice to use this gift is just that – a choice.

It's human nature to feel lost and abandoned. Believers in Jesus Christ pray for deliverance in times of trouble and ask him for help to get through difficult circumstances. All over the world people want deliverance from grief, hunger, mental illness, famine, abuse, captivity, and so much more. This world can be brutal, and mankind needs all the spiritual help we can get. A breakthrough occurs when we overcome a breakdown and find strength to endure any situation.

According to Scripture, our Spirit Father sent Jesus back into the earth to be our "deliverer." He did this to create awareness that goodness is the opposite of evil. Jesus had to die a human death in order for goodness to overcome the evil that hated him, beat him, and nailed him to a cross to die. Evil and goodness cannot coexist in the same space at the same time. Jesus loved and forgave his enemies. When Jesus died on the cross, his true *self* returned to the spirit realm. Humanity had to die in order for the Holy Spirit to be sent to us so our Spirit Father's power can work through us. We believers can only receive the fruit of the Spirit if we believe Jesus Christ is the spirit savior. The fruit is not just words, but actions. The words have to be expressed in a Christ-like character. Let me put it another way so you can better understand. You have to think the right way to do right.

If you want to win a foot race, you have to be equipped to be a good runner. An athlete who is a beginner has a different level of experience than a seasoned runner. It's simply impossible to win a gold medal when the mind and body are not in condition to compete. Levels of physical and mental development are obvious when it comes to sports, but what about inner growth? What about levels of faith? Not every believer is the master of their own destiny or is mature in their walk. Without exercising the fruit of the Spirit we lose effectiveness.

Look back at the personal core values exercise in Step Three. It's important to know what makes you YOU! When you look at the personal core values you checked, what five things did you value most? List them here as a reminder.

1. _____
2. _____
3. _____
4. _____
5. _____

Personal values are stated in simple words like wealth, honesty, success, equality, brotherly love, etc. Keep in mind that different values work for different people. You and I have different values that make us unique as individuals. Although we both have the same Spirit Father, we are different in the way we look at life and live it.

Core personal values are what define the essence of how we live. Every individual has a list of core values. These are deeply held beliefs that influence what we most want to achieve during our lifetime on earth. And while our circumstances may change year after year, our core personal values are constant and deeply rooted. Evaluate the five things on the previous page that are important to you. Do any of your values reflect a righteous direction in your life? For example, someone who is always trying to do the right thing may value integrity.

Now let's go to the end of Step Three to better understand what I mean. In the exercise, you selected negative behaviors that are holding you back. I want you to think deeply about the impact each of these behaviors has on your life. Write what you think would have happened in certain situations if you had acted differently.

_____

_____

Okay, you now have two valuable pieces of information about yourself: your personal core values and behavior that's holding you back. The purpose of this seventh step is to create a breakthrough in your life. If something isn't working, consider all the things you can change and take responsibility to make it happen. Stop repeating the same mistakes over and over again. Consider the one area where you need to make the biggest change and commit yourself to do it.

Emotional maturity is a process we all go through to acquire the ability to manage our emotions so we can make better decisions. Seeking to understand something without involving emotions is very hard. We need help from a deep inner source to control our actions and reactions. After reviewing your negative behaviors in Step Three, would you say your emotional intelligence is high or low?

When you are aware of different aspects of your own personality, you can choose to move your soul (mind, emotion, and spirit) to a new level of life. Or you can choose to stay where you are and be a victim of worldly forces. Ask yourself this question: If I could change just one thing in my life, what would it be?

Knowing that you can change something gives hope to the meaning of life. What all humans have in common is our ability to think, to learn, and to decide how we want to grow and mature while on this journey called life. We may be different in the language we speak, the color of our skin, the texture of our hair – but all humans are the same in our creation. The key to happiness is what we decide to change and how we decide to live intentionally. So, start thinking in terms of breakthrough.

With self-awareness we have freedom to decide what to do about our negative habits. We can choose to suppress them so they become dormant and undeveloped in our subconscious mind; or we can accept them as part of our individual personality. If we ask Jesus to help us use our talents to help others, something amazing happens. I can't explain it, but I certainly can testify to a higher power that changed me. If you are sincere, and call on Jesus, he will answer.

Like most people, I have embarrassing moments in my past. I became so caught up in the world that my soul was totally out of alignment with the spirit realm. I was wishing and whining instead of praising and praying. When I took the time to look back at my life, I could honestly see many things I had done wrong. I was the victim of my own making. Again, awareness is everything. I knew my change had to come from the inside. I made a commitment to learn from every experience and make wiser decisions.

I hope this book has been as much of an "AH-HA MOMENT" for you as it has been for me. I gained so much knowledge simply by writing it as my testimony. Many of life's anxieties come from being narrow-minded in our thoughts and limited in our life focus. But when we're being true to ourselves, when we take responsibility for our actions and do what really matters, we are living with purpose.

Hopefully you're now ready for a life-changing experience. Our Spirit Father has a specific purpose for the life of every person He creates. For me, it's using my talents and skills to help other people, especially teens and young adults, discover and explore the path to a meaningful life. We humans must put our Spirit Father first and follow the path He sets before us. Imagine how different the world would be if everyone recognized and used their talents to do something good. Living a godly life is based on common sense.

The good news is that our Spirit Father doesn't expect us to fulfill His purpose on our own. Humans simply don't have that kind of ability. Without the indwelling presence of Jesus Christ, old habits in the subconscious mind will continue to be in control our actions.

Above all, know that you don't have to be an emotional hostage to worldly circumstances. Anger, doubt, fear, depression, self-pity, and more must be disciplined and controlled by the soul (mind, emotions, and free will). Knowing this and drawing on inner strength is necessary to move from a flesh-led life to a spirit-led life.

New believers often think they need more of Jesus to be able to cope with difficult circumstances and situations. Truthfully, every Christian has all the Jesus he or she will ever need. None of us has more of the indwelling fruit of the Spirit than the other. Some of us simply view problems from a different perspective. Anyone can experience growth through conflict and pain if they choose. Change is hard. As believers, Christ is our foundation. Why? Because faith in Jesus Christ is hope for these difficult times. There's a song that says, *"On Christ the solid rock I stand, all other ground is sinking sand."* What is the foundation you are standing on?

The Bible teaches in **Hebrews 11:1 that** *faith is the substance of things hoped for, the evidence of things not seen.* Faith must be lived to have meaning. This is why Believers have a different perspective on life than nonbelievers. Following in the footsteps of Jesus is a solid foundation for having an abundant life on earth. The believer has faith that in death, Christ will transform our lowly bodies so that we will be like his immortal body, with eternal life.

I can't tell anyone how to live their life. But to live wisely, we must continuously push ourselves to think realistically about our circumstances and situations. The physical world is very complex.

A breakthrough is not going to come automatically. It comes by reading the Bible every day, by praying every day, and by simply caring about other people. The believer must be like the athlete who wants a gold medal. It means preparing the soul and the spirit to win. How? Well, to start, we have to be accountable for any hurt or harm done to others. Would you like to be forgiven by our Sprit Father for any evil you've done? This is the only way you will be able to move from your now to your next level of spiritual growth.

It's one thing to say, "I'm sorry" and another thing to be forgiven. Examine your conscience. Be sincerely sorry for things you have done to others that you should not have done. If you want change to happen, take little steps regularly each day to be a better person.

To receive pure love and forgiveness is a blessing. Simply accept the invitation Jesus is extending to you right now. There's no other way to begin a relationship with our Spirit Father. You can't do it on your own. If Jesus is calling; if he's speaking to your heart, go ahead and answer him. Say this confession to yourself or speak it out loud.

Almighty Father,

I believe you created me to have a personal relationship with you. I also believe I must be born again in the Spirit. I accept Jesus Christ as my Lord and personal Savior. I know that I am a sinner and ask for your forgiveness. I believe that Jesus died on the cross for my sins and you rose him from the dead to exalt him as Christ and Lord. In the name of Jesus Christ, I thank you Father for saving me, forgiving me, and a promise of eternal life with Christ. Amen.

If you believe what you just read (or said) with all your heart, then you're ready to grow in your relationship with Jesus. This takes commitment. We are saved from being trapped in our negative thoughts which results in eternal punishment. Faith is the way we come to our Spirit Father and experience His love. We live by faith.

Commitment means you will focus all your energies and actions on being a Christian. When we belong to Christ, goodness becomes more than just a useful code of conduct; it becomes a love for and loyalty to Jesus and adoration to our Spirit Father. When faith is genuine, it becomes evident in a new attitude and behavior.

Now don't get me wrong. Our Spirit Father doesn't expect believers to be perfect like Jesus. That's impossible because we're human. In the beginning you're going to slip up as you spiral up. It's personal. Just remember Jesus is always calling us deeper into his ways. Jesus is very clear in his instructions to us. It's personal.

This is My commandment, that ye love one another as I have loved you. Greater love hath no man than this, that a man lay down his life for his friends. Ye are My friends if ye do whatsoever I command you. Henceforth I call you not servant; for the servant knoweth not what his lord doeth; but I have called you friends, for all things that I heard from My Father I have made known to you. Ye have not chosen Me, but I chose you and ordained you that ye should go and bear fruit, and that your fruit should remain: that whatever ye shall ask the Father in My name, he may give it to you. These things I command you, that ye love one another.
– John 15:12-17 (KJV)

Believers who commit to this task find favor with our Spirit Father. That's not just a promise, it's Truth. Of course, that doesn't mean believers will avoid the harsh realities of the world. Trouble will always come. Only our Spirit Father can control the attitudes and behaviors of ungodly people. He also controls the forces of nature that bring destructive winds, rain, and wildfires. The world is unpredictable, and we humans are vulnerable.

What we can count on is a Spirit Father and a Savior who are always with us and will provide whatever we need. Notice I didn't say give us what we want; I said provide what we need. So don't start out by asking for a Mercedes Benz in the name of Jesus. While I'm not suggesting you need to eliminate things you want when you pray, the quality of your prayer is very important.

Even the disciples asked Jesus how to pray. Only when you recognize the power of prayer can you begin to understand the significance of a prayerful life.

- Prayer is the most powerful tool for personal transformation.
- Prayer is designed for you to appreciate the grace and mercy you receive daily from our Spirit Father.
- Prayer guides behavior and choice through the Holy Spirit.
- Prayer reminds us to value what is spiritual.
- Prayer acknowledges the authority of our Father over creation.

Moments of prayer are not enough. This is something Jesus knew well. He humbled himself constantly to God receive power; to be a miracle worker; and receive strength to endure temptation. Jesus provided us with a pattern for prayer that is found in every version of the Bible, in Mathew 6:9-13. All Jesus did was demonstrate how to have a conversation with our Spirit Father, who hears every word and request. There are many versions of this prayer in English.

Jesus tells us in Mathew 6:9-15 to build a relationship with our Spirit Father. This is how we should communicate with Him.

Our Father, who art in heaven, hallowed be thy name. Thy kingdom come; thy will be done in earth as it is in heaven.

Give us today our daily bread. And forgive us our debts (sins) as we forgive our debtors (those who sin against us).

Lead us not into temptation but deliver us from evil. For thine is the kingdom, and the power, and the glory forever. Amen.

We are n instructed to praise Him (Worship Him) for who He is and thank Him (Be Grateful) for what He does. Psalm 104:1-4

We should be sorry (Confess Wrongdoings) for our sins and ask Him for forgiveness. Psalm 51:1-2

We should remember to pray for others (Petition) and while we're at it, pray for ourselves. If there's a request, we should ask humbly in Jesus' name. Philippians 4:6-7

A transformation happens when we place Jesus at the center of our life, instead of letting circumstances and situations dictate our actions. In Matthew 6:6-7, Jesus provides instruction on how to pray. *But you, when you pray, go into your room, and when you have shut the door, pray to your Father who is in the secret place; and your Father who sees in secret will reward you openly.*

This simple guide shows us how to have a conversation with our Spirit Father. The Bible says the Holy Spirit helps us to know what to say and how to say it. We should never ignore the role the Holy Spirit plays. So, let's explore the identity of the Holy Spirit.

The blessings of faith; the experiences of love, and the joy of hope provide us with evidence of spiritual realities. The Holy Spirit is the resurrected Jesus. Our Spirit Father wants to produce His character in every human being He creates. The seed that He plants in the heart is already the image of an ideal person. By His grace and through the power of the Holy Spirit you can become your true self—a complete spiritual being living in a human body.

Again, the most important thing to remember about making this journey is that it takes time. Avoid the temptation to quit. Our Spirit Father doesn't not expect you to live a spiritual life using sheer human power – *it's impossible!* Jesus knew this; he was human. If it were possible for us to transform ourselves, our spirit Father would not have sent us an anointed helper.

Jesus said in John 16:7 – *"Nevertheless I tell you the truth; it is expedient for you that I go away; for if I go not away, the Comforter will not come unto you; but if I go, I will send Him to you."*

The journey down the path to eternal life isn't easy. Do whatever you can to create a special "My Space" where you can read the Bible and pray. Trust me, it is worth the effort to do this daily. You can't have a breakthrough without help from the Holy Spirit.

The Bible has any examples of ordinary people accomplishing extraordinary things throughout history. In Genesis, we see the story of Joseph being sold into slavery by his brothers when he was seventeen years old. Joseph found favor with our Spirit Father who had a plan for him. Joseph had a prophetic gift. He could interpret dreams. Pharaoh's dream about cows and stalks of grain befuddled his most skilled counselors. But Joseph, in his wisdom, gave God credit for his interpretation of the dream. Joseph found favor with the Egyptian Pharoah and by the time he was age thirty he had an important position as vice regent and a title of "Prince." Joseph forgave his bothers and brought the Israelites to Egypt. Centuries later, a Pharoah who didn't know Joseph saw a growing population of Hebrews as a threat to Egypt and decided to enslave them. This was evil. Our Spirit Father heard the cries of His chosen people, who were being treated harshly by the Egyptians for more than 430 years.

In the book of Exodus, we see the intent of our Spirit Father's work when he calls Moses, a Hebrew raised by the Egyptians, to set 600,000 Hebrew captives free. This is evidence of yet another spiritual reality. One man led over a half million people through the Red Sea. They were on their way to the "Promised Land."

When Moses brought the Hebrew slaves out of Egypt, they were a hot mess. There was no Old Testament for them to read; no rules for them to live by. Their animal nature was the only thing they knew.

As a nation, the Israelites were our Spirit Father's chosen people, destined to bless the world. But at the time, they had been enslaved for more than 400 years. I can only imagine how they behaved after being stripped of their culture, dignity, and self-esteem.

For forty years the Israelites wandered in the wilderness, while Moses took them to a new level of thinking, starting with the ten commandments. Moses never made it into the "land of milk and honey" that was promised to his ancestor, Abraham; but the Israelites did. The escape of the Hebrew people from Egypt is still celebrated by Jews every year in the Festival of Passover.

In 1 Samuel, the Bible tells the story of David. He wasn't born into royalty, yet he rose from the status of a shepherd to become a King. David had a musical gift of playing the harp.

Our Spirit Father sent the prophet Samuel to Bethlehem to find the next young leader for King Saul's court. His plan was to bring David and his harp to Bethlehem for a purpose.

Whenever the King fell into a mood of despair, he would send for David whose singing and harp playing brought peace and comfort. The prophet Samuel anointed David as the King who would succeed Saul on the throne. Even as King, David never stopped singing and playing his harp.

During his reign, David wrote many of the poetic verses found in the book of Psalms. He was succeeded on the throne by his son Solomon who wrote Psalms as well as the book of Proverbs. King Solomon is still considered one of the wisest men who ever lived.

In the final analysis you must ask yourselves—what does my Spiritual Father want from me? What does He expect me to do? Why does He want me to grow spiritually? The answer is simple. He loves you unconditionally and wants you to do the same for others. Quite like the disciples, you are called to live out your values in this earthly dimension. The secret to achieving a balance of body, soul and spirit is to make sure the things you care about most don't conflict with our Spirit Father's will.

Trust The Journey

You've heard the saying, "Life is short." Well, it really is. Making the best of your time on earth is critical if you believe there's a final judgement and an eternal life with Jesus. Frankly, I believe in the truth of the New Testament. That's why I wrote this book as my testimony, the story of my Christian journey. I can only hope that it has inspired you to become a witness with a testimony of your own.

There is no such thing as a perfect human life on earth. No matter how good a person may be, they can never be perfect. The journey will always have bumps in the road, with ups and downs and highs and lows. The experiences and lessons learned help us to grow into the person we are destined to become. Most important, our final resting place depends on the choices we've made along the way.

I've learned to think of life as an adventure with *self*, constantly moving through different phases as I've grown older and wiser.

The seven steps in this book took me out of my comfort zone while I was writing. In my younger life, I wasn't aware of *self*. Now I'm on a path that has purpose and meaning. As I moved to higher levels of consciousness, during this journey with you, I came to the realization that my Spirit Father is always bringing me back to Him.

We come into the world as spirit and this is how we return to our Spirit Father. The seven steps in this book are what provided me with the inspiration to kick-start my own life-changing journey. Once I became aware of my flaws and strengths, my perception of being human changed. My value system changed. I had a new mindset. My positive thoughts turned into positive actions.

Progress comes in steps. So, if you're thinking about taking the path toward a more meaningful life, you don't have to do it alone. Personally, I know from experience that change can be difficult when you come to an internal crossroad. You have to decide which path to take. Leaving the familiar to go to the unknown isn't an easy choice. Not everyone decides to follow Jesus.

I believe the true meaning of life relates to a purpose for living. Always keep in mind that we are spirit having a human experience. Identifying *self* as spirit is difficult because we see ourselves as a living body in a physical world. We can't see ourselves as spirit with purpose unless we understand the inseparable connection with our Spirit Father. These seven steps are just the beginning of a basic life pursuit of who we would really are. If you want change to happen, you must focus on what is most important to you as a spirit being.

In **Step One** we learned that matter is substance. To live well, it is necessary to understand the reality of this worldly dimension as best you can. Life is often painful because humans tend to avoid reality. We waste energy trying to enjoy the illusion of a good life. Yet, it's how we all learn best—making decisions and then experiencing the results of our choices. It's through these life experiences that we begin to question the purpose and meaning of our existence.

Step Two introduced you to a Spirit Father who formed you as spirit before you were created as a human being in your mother's womb. Everything you are today existed as a divine idea before you were born. This was our Spirit Father's plan so you could experience the world for yourself. What makes you different from everything else He created is your ability to think and to reason. You discovered who *self* really is. – a spirit having a human experience.

In **Step Three**, you gained knowledge that the soul is how the physical body experiences life. We reviewed the key elements of the inner soul, and you are now aware of how the mind, emotions, and free will are interconnected with a human sensory system in the body. You identified your personal values as well as subconscious habits that are holding you back from spiritual growth. You are more aware of self in the now and people see you as you really are.

Step Four was another awakening. During this step you were able to evaluate your emotional intelligence. More important, you were able to see how the brain controls awareness of an individual's ongoing experiences, which in turn influences thought and behavior patterns. You learned that you are what you think. You also learned that *self* is at the inner core of your human nature, growing you from the inside out, into the fullness of your spiritual being. Life is worth living if you know how to live.

Step Five took our journey on a giant leap down another path of spiritual awareness. You were able to understand the uniqueness of your creation and the value of your humanity. You learned that character is shaped by your beliefs and view of the world, while personality describes attitude and behavior. More important, you learned how Jesus had a dual nature which was both human and divine. He is truly one of a kind.

As Divine Spirit, Jesus had the authority of our Spirit Father to control his environment and perform miracles. We also learned that Jesus became the human sacrifice to show us the inner life is greater than the human life. If our time here on earth doesn't have purpose, then a life is wasted, and our living has been in vain.

Step Six takes a deep dive into the spiritual realm to learn the difference between the human nature of Jesus and the divine nature of Christ. What we learned in this step is that Jesus was the son of man (fully human). He was also a divine creation (fully spirit), meaning a part of our Spirit Father had become flesh. Different views of this have been debated for thousands of years, but what matters most is what you believe. Jesus died an earthly death as a human being so we could have evidence of our eternal destination as spirit.

And finally, **Step Seven** is about breaking through the barriers of doubt to live more in line with spiritual values. If you understand your beginning, which is spirit, and your ending, which is spirit returning to our Spirit Father for eternal life, then my job is done.

After reading this book you may be at a crossroad. It's a point in your life where you must decide which path to take. Remember, you have a choice. The decision can lead to positive results or something negative. Situations aren't going to go away. You'll just know how to deal with them better.

If you're still with me, you've made the decision to give up a complicated life. You've made a confession, and you know how to pray. Throughout this seven-step journey you have read about the human process of spiritual growth. Hopefully, you've discovered a need to evolve to higher-order thinking for self-management.

Bible study and prayer are essential for spiritual growth. They nourish the soul. There are values in the Old and New Testaments that are necessary for developing a Jesus character. The more we spend time studying the Bible (not just reading, but understanding the passages), the more your conscious mind can apply wisdom that gives basic guidance for a more fruitful life.

As Christians, we are commanded by Jesus to exhibit responsible behavior, live to glorify our Spirit Father, and enrich society with service. The Bible was written by men inspired by our Spirit Father for this very purpose, to nurture the moral and spiritual life of mankind. I call it **B**asic **I**nstructions **B**efore **L**eaving **E**arth.

Meet The Author

Creative, empowering, and inspiring are how some people describe Joan Carroll-Flowers. As a marketing specialist, she spent more than two decades creating award-winning campaigns for major brands. After calling it quits in the world of advertising, she become an award-winning entrepreneur and business consultant.

During the next two decades of her journey, Joan authored and published 10 books, including the *Black Male Crisis* and *The Black College Career Guide*. As a curriculum specialist, she has created and implemented project learning programs for schools in underserved areas and nonprofits that engage youth in life-changing learning.

After piloting a methodology to advance sustainability concepts in corporate and government supply chains, she created an award-winning certification called SEMS™ (Small Enterprise Managing Sustainability). The City of Cincinnati recognized her for training hundreds of small and diverse businesses to have a competitive advantage in the climate economy.

In 2017, the U.S. Department of Housing and Urban Development (HUD) recognized SEMS™ as a "national best practice" for economic inclusion on sustainable construction and rehabilitation of RAD federally funded housing projects. SEMS™ training improved the operations of Section 3 small and diverse vendors and won awards for the Cincinnati Metropolitan Housing Authority.

Today, Joan is on a mission to fulfill a purpose greater than herself. At a time when young people are experiencing an unprecedented mental health crisis, she is working to help teens and young adults living in marginalized communities to rise above their circumstances. The purpose of her books, *The People Zoo: A Guide To Know Who You're Talking To* and *The Deliverance Project* is to provide interventions that prevent juvenile arrests and recidivism. She offers the opportunity for experienced trainers to be licensed agents to use her learning programs.

Made in the USA
Middletown, DE
04 September 2024

60281122R00076